LEAVE LUCK TO HEAVEN

Brian Oliu

UNCANNY VALLEY PRESS

for mom & dad

who bought me countless games

who patiently watched me fall into pits/get crushed by falling ceilings/mistime the Bull Charge

who waited out many "hold on, it's my last life"s

and, above all, who loved me unconditionally

thank you.

LIBRARY OF CONGRESS CATALOGING-IN-PUBLICATION
DATA AVAILABLE UPON REQUEST

ISBN 978-1-934819-99-9

Cover art by David Wells
Design by Mike Meginnis

Published by Uncanny Valley Press
www.uncannyvalleypress.com

CONTENTS

Super Mario Bros., 13

Rad Racer, 16

Maniac Mansion, 19

Leave Luck to Heaven Walkthrough, 22

River City Ransom, 25

Save Point: Children's Song Park, 28

Adventure Island, 30

Metroid, 33

Boss Battle: The One with the Long Neck, 36

Bubble Bobble, 38

Double Dribble, 41

Wizards and Warriors, 44

Plants, Flowers, Vines, 47

Super Mario Bros. 2, 50

Save Point: The Inn, 54

Rampage, 57

Shadowgate, 60

Boss Battle: A Woman Made of Feathers, 64

Ninja Gaiden, 66

Ninja Gaiden II, 67

Ninja Gaiden III, 70

1up, 72

Simon's Quest, 75

Zelda II: The Adventure of Link, 79

>>>, 82

Contra, 84

Balloon Fight, 87

Boss Battle: The Eye from Which We See Ourselves, 90

Donkey Kong, 92

Goonies II, 95

Boss Battle: The Thing That Burrows Up to Greet Us, 98

Dragon Warrior, 100

Punch-Out!!, 103

Super Mario Bros. 3, 106

Boss Battle: The Gold Robot, 110

Gradius, 112

Kid Icarus, 115

R.B.I. Baseball, 118

Boss Battle: The Death of the Caterpillar, 122

Tetris, 124

Mega Man 2, 127

Save Point: The Church, 130

Tecmo Super Bowl, 131

Ghosts 'N Goblins, 134

Boss Battle: The Girl I Was Supposed to Save, 140

Friday the 13th, 142

Blaster Master, 145

Boss Battle: My Brother Who Controls the Weather, 148

Save Point: Hot Springs, 150

The Final Boss, 152

"There are secrets where fairies don't live."
—*Old Man, Legend of Zelda*

LEAVE LUCK

TO HEAVEN

SUPER MARIO BROS.

Thank you, but the princess is in another castle. We are sorry, but
the princess is in another castle. We are sorry. We are sorry, we are
so sorry for all of this. Please accept our apology. We are so sorry.
We know how far you have come. We are sorry things have gotten
complicated. We would've told you about the time it snowed, but
no one saw it. We would've told you about the time the fire spun
underwater, but the squid are the only things that can swim. We
would've told you when the sky changed from pale blue to white-
black that it meant something, that you were close, that the sky is
not the only thing that changes. We would've told you being indoors
meant something. We are sorry. We are sorry, thank you. We know
you stood on a porch in a city in a world that you just met and the sky
changed. We know that you thought it would be different. We know
that it rained. We know about the cascading. We know how fast you
ran, how little time it took to get here. We know about the fireworks
over the church, over the chapel, and how the sound never synched
up to the blasts. We know about the building named after a saint and
the piano inside it. We know how you would practice. We are sorry
for this. We know how you got from one place to another—how the

world gets interrupted. We know how you interrupt the world. We know that this world would not exist without you. Thank you.

Thank you, but the princess is in another castle. Thank you, but the princess is in another princess. We are sorry, but the princess is in another princess in another castle. We are sorry, but the princess is in another princess in another castle in another castle. The castle in another castle is made of brick the color of mint, the color of nothing, the color of your eyes, maybe. The color of the eyes of the princess inside the princess change according to her mood—according to your story. You have not seen them in a while—they might have changed while you were running, while you were outside. The morning after the night you made a promise you broke that promise. The trick is to keep moving. The trick is to know when to stop, when to push your body forward like you are trying to make yourself fall, like you are pretending not to notice the edge. We saw the pause: we saw you frozen above the pit, suspended. We looked on. We are sorry for staring. We are sorry that you're not laughing. We saw you run too fast. We saw the dirt kick up from untied shoes, from feet not yet formed. We saw your arm lie dead at your side while the other swung like a champion. Run to here and then back. Run around this tree. Touch the chain-link fence with your left hand. Hear it shake. We are sorry, but we know you can never catch up. We are sorry. To watch you run made us laugh: the shortness of your legs and how they can barely carry you. Your timing is horrid: it is such a horrible thing. Pause. This is as fast as you can go and we are sorry. We are sorry, but the castle is in another princess. Inside the castle inside the princess the weeds are tall but dead. We should've told you that the fire is able to

14

hold hands, to link together and form something taller, something larger than you can imagine. You see these things all the time. We know. We know you can explain how things work: the method, the pattern.

We ask you to take pause. We ask you to think of it this way, for once. Think of your legs moving up and down like pistons, like dead plants. Think of the world moving in a straight line from right to left. Think about the time it rained crow's feet. Think of how the spikes moved, how they floated behind you the faster you ran. Think of the dream where you ran so fast you levitated. Think of how slowly you moved: your feet unable to push off of the ground, over the sharp points. Think of how you can be chased while standing still. Start thinking this way. The ground everywhere is made of rock: all the grass is dead. We give you thanks.

RAD RACER

At night, the city in the distance never gets any closer, despite bodies going as fast as the bits would allow—the number synonymous with the south-pointing chariot, the wheels turning without magnets. The measurements of solar time are perfect provided there are no curves in the road, and there aren't for some time; a straight shot from where we once were to where we are going, the lines in the road glowing green like the lights in the windows of the buildings of the city I will never get to. The land where I am from is synonymous with transport economics; you will know me by where you slow down—the roads get more intricate in their curves and stops: they are known by numbers, they are known by the names of dead farmers and soldiers, the names of crops that died so that you can admire what is left of the barley as you wonder why the roads are lined with trees. The road bends around us—we see a hill and turn off the car to let the ghosts push our weight. This wheel dictates where I appear. The lights turn when I turn. There are no lights here—only the negatives of things. All colors reversed. The colors change and divide to provide more depth, to let us see the cars coming at us faster and with more ridges on their bodies, to make the flips and crashes real. If you stare at one color long enough your eyes will get fatigued and your brain will forget that color exists. On Saturday mornings I would lay in my bed that my father had built. This bed is a boat. This bed is not a car. I would convince myself that when I could sit in the front seat without feeling sick to my stomach we would catch up to time—that I could press a button that would take me to my grandmother's house, where I could stay the night and she would make me eggs in the morning. The car, which is not a car, is green and seats only me; my parents are dead now, but I must keep the house in order. I must steer the tractor; I must learn how to put the blades down so the grass won't get too long. We might have a dog now and he needs to eat. In my car that is not a car I fall asleep. The wheels move with the road—it can read all of the signs; it knows all of the turns. When the car is upside down like a dead bird, there is no one in the car. There is no broken glass, no dent in the door where I would try to get out. The car will right itself and slide back onto the road like tires on ice into the grille of a truck on my way to school. It is January and you thought about speed and lampposts. When I wake up it is raining and the time is up and there is no movement. In the dream where I wake up I am in my father's car and no one is driving. My parents are on the front steps and they are waving goodbye as I try to open the door to get out. There is a dead quail on the side of the road. The car that no one is driving will never stop driving. There is my house again. There are my parents again. There is a dead quail on the side of the road. There is my house again. There are my parents screaming. There is a dead quail on the side of the road. There is my house, off-yellow with blue shutters and a blue door, which is open. My mother is reading a book. My father is mowing the lawn. We know that things are moving when they are not moving—we will disappear like lilacs when it is our turn.

MANIAC MANSION

We are all here, and we are all here together with our backs to the moon. Here is a house. Go to it. Go to door. Open door. The door is locked and you should've known. There is a key beneath the doormat, and you should've known. When I was young there were plants that lined our walkway. One day I saw a snake move from one plant to another and disappear like a light being turned off, a coil of green spit from the leaves. At school, I told the children that it was poisonous, that I reached my hand into the leaves to get the key we kept hidden in the mulch so I could open the door and run upstairs without saying hello to my mother because she is not home. I can run up those stairs faster than anyone—hands over feet. This is the house I grew up in. There were fourteen stairs that I counted every time I ran down them. In my sleep I crawled up bookcases, feet touching pages documenting how to make a rocket, lessons on giving, lessons on not giving. Go to sleep. Open sleep. There is a photograph of me standing in front of the door on my way to school. I cannot remember how our kitchen looked. I cannot remember how our bathroom looked. I used to live in a hallway. My bed was a boat and I would draw on the windows in crayon mornings before church, before I was lifted up from under my arms and brought down to the ground. Pick up child. I was in love with insulation but it made me itch. There are sheets for my bed. There is a cast for my arm. I would sit in the darkness of the attic to learn what darkness is. We cannot use the word *kill*. It must be changed. There are neighbors here. The man next door is named red. They have a white dog and I have given it a new name. There is a girl who says the devil lives in her room but her mother got rid of it. There is a farm and sometimes the quails escape. Everyone within a five-mile radius is going to die if I press the button. This is where the magic happens. This is where the heart is. Ring the doorbell. The door is locked and you should've known. My mother's not a person—she is my mother. They are a building a house nearby. My father's not a person—he is my father. I threw rocks in the air and I hurt someone. They are not people—they should be home and they are not. There is no key hidden here; this is not a home. I would come here, amongst the grey siding and garbage dumpsters, the wooden stairs, the white walls, and collect candy. There are so many families and so little space; we could never get to them all. They gave out razor blades the kids said. They gave out apples with razor blades the kids said. Our street was named after a bird that I had never heard of, a kingbird, a tyrant. A hockey game swirls on cinder blocks and we are sad. There was no basement here, no attic. Go to loose brick. You learn quickly that you can operate at one speed here; there is no button to hold down to make legs to move faster. There is no outrunning the nurse at the refrigerator. There is no getting to the door. There is a strategy here that involves the hero getting caught and pressing the brick and trying to run for the door. Go to door. The door is locked and you should've known. There are three of us. Press the brick and let the other out. I remember nothing about the house I lived in before I lived there. There is a photograph I have seen of me holding my body up by pressing my hand into a wall. It is dark; there is a light. This is where I lived, at the end of this hallway. My first memory was not this. Stand by the brick and press the brick. I am not scared of the dark. There is no gas for the chainsaw. In this house that is not a house is a grandfather clock that moves like a terror. The boy with blue skin has the same name as my father. The boy with blue skin has the same name as a town that I know. I know the color blue. There is no way to document this. There are numbers that need to be written down—I have memorized my phone number and it has not changed despite changes in ceilings. I want you to come to my house. Please come to my house. I am proud of you, House. There is a cheerleader in my house. There is a bully in my house. We will learn about the beatitudes and they will eat my dessert; they will watch my television. My mother has cleaned the basement. There is a new coat of paint on the walls. This house is growing smaller with every new color. The deck is peeling. There is a hole where the horse went through. I was the only one home when it happened. There were no dogs. This house looks smaller without walls. My room exists without walls. My father and I stuff wires into electric boxes and eat soup cooked on a fire. We press tiles onto the floor while watching television. The sawdust sticks to our shirts. We see the dogs. A horse walked up to our door. Go to door, horse. The horse's leg snapped—I heard it crack like a tree, like peppermint. I was home. Walk to. What is.

LEAVE LUCK TO HEAVEN WALKTHROUGH

In my grandmother's house, there was no paint, just wooden walls and night-lights: I would run my finger across the paneling to feel my way to where my grandparents were watching television: loud gunshots and fire-eyed speeches, words I would never understand. A memory and nothing afterward—a snap and then sleep.

Afterward, a house with the snake in the front yard. Afterward, a house where I don't remember the first moments: the moving in, the unpacking of boxes. I don't remember having a say—your bed goes here, upstairs. Your bed is next to the attic with the pink puffs of insulation. I wanted to touch it, but it was made of glass, it would keep us warm. I know you know this but I had trouble sleeping—I wanted it to be colder than you could imagine. I want the window open. I am safe when I hold your hand and cross the street. I am safe when I am in my house. The car, fast, could not hit us—it would pass through us like a ghost, like a blowing curtain. I am going to tell you where I would hide if you found the key under our doormat. If you found the key under our doormat, my mother would lock you in the basement. My mother did not paint things back then. My father did not build things back then. We did not care about furniture, about sconces, about recessed lighting. This lamp provides light. You can sit on the ground if you'd like. This house is not ours. It never was: the smells of cooked pork from the downstairs neighbor, the wiring on the windows. There were no hiding places—no bookshelf that would rotate, no brick to push to open the door. No one would visit.

Afterward, a house that always changes. My mother jokes that long after we are gone from Earth, long after the people that inhabit the scorched Earth understand what a house is and what it looked like, they will find the remnants of a building underneath the dirt and ash and know that it is old. Many years after that, they will try to figure out how old—how did the people in this house live, what rooms did they sleep in, what rooms did they keep hidden from guests. They will think the house is older than it is: they will not understand that style is modern—that to evolve from Queen Anne, there would have to have been a Queen Anne: arm slouched, a hybrid of thistle and rose sprouting from the same stem. This house is ours, and we can change it when we want: the dark red in the foyer a custard yellow now, after primer and three coats of white. The light taupe in the kitchen, the color of a mouse's back, has been replaced with yellow. All things yellow. All things no longer permanent—the lighting up of the room, springtime when it is winter, certainly—but we are in New Jersey; the house set back into the woods separated by fences that keep the horses from cutting through our yard and eating the fake apples off the summer wreath, so that their legs cannot burst through the wooden planks of our porch (my father and I laid them down, slat by slat, painted them battleship grey with a touch of blue, summer, spring, lighter) and snap in two with no way to set the bone. I don't want to think about the most humane way to kill a horse, but I will: a poisoned meal, a bullet between the eyes, a freezing. My grandmother used to bet on the horses as a child and on the larger races she still does. She sends a card in the beginning of May. Inside there are folded bills, and the words *your horse came in*. I wonder how she picked my horse, if it was random or if the horse looked like me, broad-bodied and slow. If that is the case I don't know how I could ever win—I would be a horse that carried wood to the barn. I would be the horse with the broken leg that you would try to drown in a bucket of water. To win: leave. To win, know this house is not a house where anyone could live. To win, know that these things serve a purpose—a stone in the basement, an attempt to make music, an attempt to make the world love what is left.

RIVER CITY RANSOM

The sound of the shuttering of the store behind where you are standing is the sound of the subway car as it gets closer to the station. I imagine you underground most evenings, though you could've walked from place to place—always left to right, always east. There will be doors, later. There will be woods and patches of water to jump over lest we lose everything. There will be warehouses and junk-yards and you will run through them—people will move diagonally toward you to look and you will be too fast. When you were young the trucks would park in front of the brownstones and you would pay a quarter to touch the tree branches. When you were young, a boy lost his arm in the limbs. These are the stories that I hear: about twirling fire, about breaking both of your arms. These are the things that happened where you were and where I visit: only during the day, only when there is light coming from somewhere that is not a build-ing, that is not underground. There are transfers at city blocks—five to be exact—a grey circle switch, orange and yellow diamonds on occasion. We stop in front of the patron saint of widows, although I do not have a coin—nothing to collect but the knives and chains of people now vanished. We will carry them until they disappear from our hands like a boy in the trees, like the poison you drank from your favorite pot. Your mother slapped your back like your hands making noise against the iron and you were carried past the homes and churches after you passed out. If that was the end of things, that would be the end. Your mother had these moments too—these moments before you; the same streets, trips to the beach, though she could still see the same skyline she woke up to in the morning. There is some street name you can't remember: Church, probably. The cars are yellow because you can see them coming. There is nothing but churches, so she runs. I was almost never born, you say. You never would've been here, you say. If you were there and then not, you would wake up in a city with half of everything. You would walk into a store and buy a cup of tea. The night they could've stabbed you I can only imagine; the city has changed so much since that evening; the garage does not exist anymore, but I know you remember the spot and the cross section, you remember the light. You were beautiful, I have seen pictures, and even as I think about it now, as you sleep upstairs in a room I am familiar with, and even with the city farther away from where we are—you left there to become my mother—I have difficulty seeing you as a girl younger than I am now, emptying your purse on a cold sidewalk with a knife to your cheek. The most expensive things in the city with half of everything are words; there is only so much I can afford to learn, and I am sorry for this. I want to jump and spin in the air, to flip head over feet, to be amazing. My feet do not get faster. I am exhausted after one swing of my arm. You tell me the things I should keep after you die: this is valuable, this is important. I am not going before you, you say, and I wish I could believe it. You, your mother, her mother, her mother, her mother,

her mother, her mother, her mother, her mother survived to see a daughter, see a son, to pass on a life to me that could end on a street somewhere in between parks, at the bottom of a river. I will wake up in a city with half of everything. I will eat a tomato and my heart will stop. I will read a book and learn nothing. I will ask for a smile because that is all I can afford. You wrote letters while you were in the city. Some of them were about me, unborn. It is important to write letters, you say. You spoke for me. We are doing fine. I like apples and pickles. I do not like the buildings.

SAVE POINT: CHILDREN'S SONG PARK

We wonder how one constructs a village long before we wind up in an overgrown bamboo grove with hand-painted signs in English and Japanese urging us to push forward, to see what a song park can offer—a hidden, youthful melody that melts the hearts of sons and daughters of the devil; a song that causes hurricanes to turn counterclockwise and stops nuclei from fusing. Is there a conversation with loved ones about the sanctity of the land? Who will be the one to fill the cooler with ice and soda in order to make a quick gold coin, or diamond, or whatever currency we have been collecting off of the deaths of others? There is no leaf. There is no typewriter. There is no saving here. These are questions that perhaps were asked during the initial construction of the Children's Song Park—this crab museum that we traverse through; it is obvious that the brain trust behind such an attraction has long since packed up and left this area, perhaps even left this world all together, starting anew in some other locale, far, far away from failed plans of educating the masses on the true kings of the world and the harmonies of schoolchildren. We can imagine the park flourishing; it may flourish again after all is over; we might fly over everything after it has turned green; people we have talked to might wave; third-party vendors might sell trinkets of crustaceans and cassette tapes of classic children's songs as families dare to touch the exoskeletons of ghost crabs while admiring bronze statues of children playing baseball, the metal brought to life simply by walking past, the crackling of a sound box and the familiar instrumentation, kids holding on to soda cans and singing along. Instead, feral cats, hundreds of them, surround us, pleading in chorus to the point that they are drowning out the waves that hit the cliff nearby, joining in with the recorded songs that whisper out of an unseen speaker. We run out of the park and to a raft, a boss, a castle, our legs against cat fur. We have no way to feed any of them—we cannot stop their cries.

ADVENTURE ISLAND

Darling, let me tell you about the time I created an island. The island was a volcano once, a place where there was nothing to say but nothing—I continued forward with my face looking up toward the spiders, but my eyes were always on my feet. On the island I created, I can see through the sand to the layers of earth: a blanket on top of a blanket on top of a creature, sleeping. Please do not touch me—I will be poisoned. I will fall through the trees and into nothing, perhaps, submerged in water in which I cannot swim. I could not swim in the water so I created this island to walk across, to move from left to right, eyes to the ground. I do not know why I placed this rock here. I do not know who started this fire. During the fall, there is a bridge that will turn to dust as I walk across it—my feet destroying what my eyes created; please do not touch me. Do not feed me apples. Do not feed me bananas. I am very hungry, creating, but please don't let me eat the fruit I am creating in the trees. When you peel the orange, a spider will come out of the pulp. One leg will follow another. It will crawl up your hand like it is dancing, like you are interrupting a process. Drop the orange. Let it roll across the ground: follow it until it hits something: a snake, a snail. Do this until I stop existing. Watch me fall from the sky like a helicopter, like a cannon, like a head cut clean from its body. You must understand this—when I walk, I am not the one moving. I will create all this by standing still, by marching in place. You are fooled. You should have eaten the orange. There is no spider hiding, waiting for your hands. There is no wonder here: all of it has been replaced except for the snails. The sky, darling, is moving opposite the ground. As I move in place I move the world—I adjust the grass to my footing. In a room with no floor I die again, I roll backwards. In front of me I can touch you—I have thrown out everything I have. These things I throw move against the world—they cut in front of dead leaves and clouds, they mean nothing, I promise. When I am done with all of this, we can go outside. We can have a picnic. I will peel the orange for you. I will slice the apple. I will pull the body out of the lake, I will tell you about the time I created an island. I will tell you about other islands I have created, smaller ones. I will tell you about the people I know who have drowned. I will tell you how their bodies were found, months later. I will tell you about falling backward into the water, about the red shorts I was wearing, about taking showers, about pressing my forehead against the white tile, about my feet bleeding from where they could touch something. You shouldn't have listened. You are faster than me, but I cannot be brought down, darling, I promise. Darling, it is cold and I am wearing a hat. It was a gift from my grandmother. I will try to pull the Earth closer. I am not moving fast enough, please help me pull the Earth closer. If we can pull the Earth closer, we can punch the wasp nest, we can kick over the traps. The insects will eat the garden. They will bite at my legs. Don't listen to them. They will put holes in the fruit and then there will be nothing we can do: I cannot make more.

Darling, in my heart, there are people. In my heart there are people with torches, with axes. I will stuff them with seeds from the garden. Let me tell you about the time I created an island that was once a volcano. I will fill their mouths with it until they cannot breathe. I know this island is a line, but it is not a worm, it is not a night moth, a snail without a shell. It is not the leg of a spider bent like an elbow, like your hair on your shoulders. The shape of the island I made has nothing to do with this. It has nothing to do with an egg or the desire to go faster: if I go faster I will fall into the fire, through the trees, through the earth. The next shell I crack open, the next rind I peel could be you. We will run through the island inventing it. We will turn fire into smoke, rock into smoke, spiders into smoke. Darling, run with me until the feeling is gone.

METROID

At the end of everything there will be a heart. In this heart will be me and you and something else, although that something else is something that cannot be determined yet. I have entered from the sky. I have been walking for days, I promise—no stopping to rest, just the movement of landscape behind my body. The black moves backward while we walk forward, walk toward nothing, feet moving up and down like elevators, like transport. I wish you understood the importance of this. I wish you knew that there is more than being touched and knocked from the ground like a crown to the floor. This number used to mean something. As a child, I would roll down the stairs to the landing. I would hit the wall with a thud and run into the kitchen. It is too hot. I would put my pillow into the freezer. I can look out of the window and see you moving. On the moon, it is lonely. I would be forced to sit on its half-crescent. The moon is not big enough for you to come with me. I would say goodnight and you would not respond. Everyone is asleep where I am. This is a place I could visit. I can see you. You have red hair and you do not know where I have gone. You will wait for me for a few days longer than everyone else will. You will not sleep. When you are on your back in your bed you are talking to the sky. I cannot hear you. There is nothing to be heard here, but I am singing a song that made me cry as a child. The next day, you will tell everyone it's impossible. The next day you will find the best photograph for my funeral. I am wearing a green shirt. My face is turned so you cannot see the flash of light in my glasses. In the dark I would bite down on candy to see if I could make a spark, to create something out of nothing with the only force worth anything. My legs do not move fast enough. My arms do not move fast enough. I can jump higher here. On the moon, I know what gravity is because there is less of it. There is always less. If you tell me how much you weigh I can tell you how much you would weigh here. You would not need to worry about numbers. This says nothing about my body. This says nothing about how I look. There is nothing to eat on the moon. The moon is made of rocks and dust. If I could grow a rose here she would be beautiful. If I could grow a rose here I would shove her in my mouth. Even though you think that I am at the bottom of a reservoir you will look up at the sky to talk to me. You will tell everyone that I exist in the stars and you will not believe any of it— the words will stick to the top of your mouth like thorns. At the end of everything there is what is left of what has been stolen. At the end of everything the glass will shatter and what controls what is left will shut off. I will grow grey with the atmosphere and we must leave everything. You will think I have drowned. I used to slide down the banks of the dam on my stomach like I was victorious, like nothing you've ever seen. On the other side of the hill were ghosts who lived in the water. A jellyfish washed up on the shore once and I prodded it with a stick. I touched it with my foot and I expected to die, to have my life leave me at once like a subway car derailed by a switch in a heart in a glass jar. I thought I would lose everything. I thought I would be as zeroed as my name, but nothing happened. Nothing happened and I was cold. Nothing happened and they pointed at me and said I was sick to do such a thing, to touch what could cause me pain—that I knew better. That I knew something. I think he is swimming with the ghosts you might say. Someone has given him a fish and he has given that fish a name—my name, you might say. If I were underwater, you wouldn't hear anything. There is no need to name things here. When I run, my feet do not touch the ground. There are no ghosts where I am. There are no fish. There is no water on the moon.

BOSS BATTLE: THE ONE WITH THE LONG NECK

When I arrived, the music changed—you, queen of what remains, you in a room too small for your body. Your neck is something unfamiliar—the back of it invisible, the front of it delicate: the graze of a finger causes the chin to tilt downward, a trap, always a trap. Your face, a mask—smooth as the day you were born and hard as the stone on the ring I am wearing, the ring that allows me to pretend that this does not hurt as much as it once did, that the bruises you make fade to yellow faster, that this is what I should have always been wearing—trading the green of my youth for the color of an announcement, a declaration of danger.

You, larger than the room you have been sleeping in. You, despite this, will not push me against the wall, will not press your head into my chest, will not listen to what I am saying—that you must disappear, that the only thing that must remain is the room that we have built here: red brick, red paper, red fabric on the floor. I take my knife and start cutting—your neck breaking in sections and vanishing, tendons unraveling like our time away from this room, your neck growing shorter by the second. Your face shrinks back toward your shoulders, shoulders I remember but cannot place. You, of the neck. You, of no neck, neckless: head on body like a badly drawn picture, like something I once drew. This is where you disappear. This is where the door opens. This is all that I have wanted.

BUBBLE BOBBLE

Now it is the beginning of a fantastic story. A child, left alone, will eat everything. If we were at a point where we could name things after what our hearts are for, yours would be a vegetable never considered and outside of nature. My grandfather had a garden. This is an eggplant—purple and shiny like a bruise you never see. When I am dead, they will turn me upside down and let my skin hang until I disappear.

Cut from the vine with scissors; if you pull with your hands you will break everything. My mouth is open. My teeth are rough like fossils. The day I came to see you and broke a piece of myself in myself and swallowed it, my mouth filled with gravel. When I was a child I had no teeth. When I was a child my mouth was a cave. I will say my name once. I will count from one to ninety-nine and then over again. I will allow the onions to dry in the sun. I am named after a king. I am named after an emblem of wealth and plenty. There are crystals in my mouth I thought I could eat. There is a cross I thought I could eat. This is the journey into the cave of monsters. Unwrap this so I can feel it slide down my throat. It takes three seconds for it to reach my stomach—takes too long—and my body does not register the object—when something is inside of me, I know. The carrot I will eat has no frost on its skin. I will lick the icing from my thumb. I will eat cake. I will stack the slices on top of each other. I will reimagine what is spherical. I will lie to you about numbers and the accumulation of space. Sometimes I see myself and I am blue like sugar mixed with vanilla.

Now it is the middle of a fantastic story. Now it is the middle of a fantastic story and you wonder how I even got here. Say olive. Say olive again. My body has matched my mouth. My body has matched your mouth and I have not been paying attention. Take the floral gem and remove my core. There is nothing left to use. My stomach is greased, my liver is swollen. My teeth are topaz and you will not dance with me. I am an ambitious little boy. I am one substance in another. Let us celebrate this.

Do not lick the tears of wine. Do not eat the glass this time. This is sin. You cannot expect to live if you choose to love like this—if this love is what you live for, the popping of bubbles with people inside them, the collection of candy. The ants that spoiled a picnic I have never been on would eat the sugar in my blood. If I do not eat everything, I will feel it in my bones, in my teeth. This dread will travel through walls. It will move in straight lines like I am blessing myself. When the priest swabbed my head with his thumb the oil pooled, seeped through tissue—seeped through skin. I do not know what I am made of anymore. My skeleton is trying to kill me. What is left of me is trying to speed up time.

Now it is the end of a fantastic story. The cake that I ate on my fourth birthday is still a part of my body. When I die someone will have to bring the pastries. You will ask if anyone would like a cup of coffee. You will add milk. Those were his favorite, you will say, and everyone will nod—do you like this necklace that I found for you? I will wear it inside my throat and it will be beautiful. When the flower made out of sugar crushes my heart you will take the liquid and kill all of the plants. You will build a house and you will wash your hands in the kitchen. You will kill all of the ants. You will put my body on the fire and there will be no smoke. You will drink what is left and your lips will pucker and your mouth will ripen to a lemon. Would you like a glass of wine? Let's all have ice cream. Now, watch as I set the ground on fire.

DOUBLE DRIBBLE

The day I am unstoppable is the day you are unconscious. You should've seen me out there, running the floor like I had no concept of breath, as if I didn't understand oxidation. I never feared the pooling of blood in my feet, in my gut, or how I would walk the next day. I do not know how hard my heart works. I come in and out of view like I am invincible, intangible, here and then gone. I can make the world around me slower—you are the one slowed. I miss playing music with ensembles. I miss to the left, always. My hands that guided you home have crooked fingers and cracked palms. I rub them together and my skin comes off in black lines: these hands are dirty. This finger has been permanently fattened. This finger leans in to tell the other one a secret. The nails on the ends of these fingers are perfect. I used to clip them over the sink but the water would pool and not drain. I scatter myself across tile floors—the earth will break them down eventually—no one will notice. I hope you did not walk across those floors barefoot while I was unstoppable. I am glad I did not convince you to sleep there on the floor amongst myself: here, take this, this is mine, do not go here, here, or here. I am named after a mistake, a lapse in judgment—I thought you could be held,

41

then released, then held again. I thought I could use both hands. My favorite player died on the court. He is the same age as I am now. Our birthdays are one day apart. I lived in the city he grew up in. In the city he grew up in I would run until I collapsed: my muscles without moisture. The sinews would stiffen while I slept and it would be a struggle to get vertical, my legs strangled. The day he died my father woke me up to tell me he was dead. I wrote his name in marker on my left hand in hopes that it would make me better—that I would notice he was dead and he would tell me where to stand, where to shoot, where to jump. I did not know about the spots on the floor. I did not understand the numbers. I was too large for the shirt that separated me from the others. They would call me zero when my elbow smashed into the face of someone smaller. You know the way to my heart and when you arrive it will stop. The day that I am unstoppable I do not wake you up to let you know. The hands that could not be seen did not shake your shoulders, did not rip the twisted covers from your body to let you know that you are late for something, to let you know that there is a fire, to let you know that there is something worth standing for, that there is nothing here but you and me and that the game has ended, that there is no national anthem playing as the floods approach, that there are no balloons, that there are no colors other than the ones that we have witnessed in nature, the ones that we have created through numbers. I will be the ox. You will be the breaker. I will be the frog. You will be the eagle. I am a winner. I want you to know that I have won everything. I want you to know that I wrote your number on my wrist but the ink is swooshed across my forehead, that I have wiped my brow clean and the thumb that lingered on the circled scar on your stomach the night before I was unstoppable and you were unconscious has been jammed back into its socket. The scar that I was embarrassed to touch, every finger across the hardened bump would let you know that this was once a place of fire. This is how I would wake you up. This is how I would let you know that I know. I would tell you that the best shooter shot himself. I would tell you that the day someone I loved died I was asleep. I would tell you that the day someone I loved died I thought of my father waking me up. I thought about driving ink into my skin, scarring it, so that you would ask me about it and I could tell you about the time we tried to make baskets from across the gym—the form drilled into our head abandoned for pure power, pure chance. I would tell you that the day someone I loved died I shot baskets in the street. I would tell you that if I threw the ball overhand and without grace, I could hit the spot where he hung himself. I will not wake you up to tell you these things. I will not tell you these things when you wake up. I will flick my wrist and the ball will go through the hoop: it will not dare rattle.

WIZARDS AND WARRIORS

Let me spell it out for you: you and me sitting in a tree. You above, me below. Below, a house. Look at the map—look how high up we are, how far we need to go. Let's make our home here among the spiders, among the bees and acorns. I am making a list of the things that you love: circles, tongues. I can't tell you what this says about you. I am wearing a grey suit. I am wearing a grey suit and your skin is pink, the color of medicine. Here, take this—swallow it. I do not know how long you have been hanging in the trees. I don't know how you are suspended in midair like a gem, like a dying wasp. Somebody wrapped a string around your body. Somebody was careful with the knot. You must have raised your arms like you were dancing, like you were asking some god a question—about dead friends, about bribery. Someone pulled the string and sent you skyward. You must not have kicked. You must not have forced your weight down through your stomach and through your legs. You must not have decided to become heavy, to let the blood in your arms condense in your fingers. You must not have blood in your arms because I have seen the wounds—I have seen where a dagger of throwing or a dagger of hand has sliced perfect lines: the cuts red and raised above the pink.

Perhaps this is how you counted the days—no tree to carve lines into, four down and one across. This is how you keep count—number one repeated. If I put enough diamonds in my shoes I can get a key to the tree we are inside. I do not know who locked the door. I do not know why I can find the key in the world—amongst the owls, amongst the saints. I know you will never believe me but I saw you without your hair. I saw you without your body, thin and flushed. I saw you without your eyes, your skin. I saw what was left of you try to crush me, to build me a house to put my bones in. Let me spell it out for you. Let me tell you about a dream that I have had—you and me, sitting in a tree. You above, me below. Below, a house. Below that, you, again. Below that, you, always, always again. Soon, I will turn into a thief. Soon, I will be accepted in the city, in the house below. I will take off a helmet—I will lose what is left of my legs. I will open a window. We, the warrior, are after the enemy, the wizard. Through the door in the center of the tree is somewhere we have never been: the bees are now bats. The forest is now red. It is not fall, I promise—I promised you I would never say "fall." The tree where we have made our home is dead now—the bats weave in and out of the hole in the door. Let me cut you down from the tree—hold onto the rope as I slice, my hands around the frayed end so you don't crash to the dirt below. Before I let you down, I want you to know I cut a spirit to get here. I cut it in half like a lemon, like I was counting the days. I am here to rescue you. I am here to rescue you and you are quiet. You used to say "help"—say words that cut like diamonds when I was out of earshot, when I was in the castle, when I was underground, underneath the house, underneath you, always you. Talk to me about keys. Talk to me about bats in August the same way you talked about bugs in July. Talk

to me about diamonds, about how they spin for a second before top-
pling over. Talk about these things. The only thing I am sure of is that
the weight of my foot will kill the spider. The rest is guessing—where
to step, where my body will recognize that I am touching something,
that when I pull out a knife and press it against the rope, the rope
will break. That when you pull out a knife and press it against your
skin, your skin will break. That when your skin breaks I can see you
as nothing but a face in bone. That when I have the diamonds that
you wanted I can kick what is left of you into dust. That your spirit
will kill me. That there is no such thing as a feather that can help me
float. Here, in the tree where you count the days, I am making a list
of the things you love: circles, lines.

PLANTS, FLOWERS, VINES

If we are to catalogue these things, we must start at the beginning: even numbers, multiples of eight on days where we need them more than we would like to admit—the saving of worlds and whatnot, the remembering when we were here yet not here, the observing of our backyards and front lawns, the feeling of home. This, here, is one—one. If we are to walk outside our front door to the unfamiliar we would expect what we should always expect: a flower, green as if it had never been delicate, enamored with the world. A snapdragon, a nod to where we are going: at some point, there is a dragon, no? Fire-breathed and taller than we can ever imagine ourselves being: spikes as crisp as crystal, a digitized roar like a crackled speaker. At some point, we put their hands in the dragon's mouth to demonstrate their lack of fear, their certainty— that its jaws would never snap closed, just like when we are close to home there is nothing that can hurt us: we know where the water runs, we know where the wasp nest hides.

Inside of us is a buzzing of bees, rotating their wings like a child's song, like hands sharpening knives. Most days they are in our heads, whispering to each other when thoughts turn to something other than chrysanthemums—petals extending out into circles like echoes, like a stone thrown into the water. We think of the spider and its web—fragile, certainly, spun sugar dresses and compartments, a terror reserved for the tests of saints. Later, a spider. Later, legs that sprawl out like bony elbows, like hands asking, wanting. A spider is a flower that has fallen open—petals intact until it is time for the shattering.

Long after the breaking, a return to familiar form: you, gone from before—the familiar flash, then nothing but an empty room, doors open. Someone found you. I thought you were in the ground, but someone found you and put you back together: arms where they should be, hair pushed back. We are further from home now—the numbers like soft steps, and you don't belong here. When they brought you back, they dipped you in paint—before, you were white. Before, you were a pink clove. When tears hit the soil, there was you left behind: you, red, on the last day of May. You are green now.

There will be a time where it will be you but it does not look like you. The green will fade to something sickly—something that was but is no longer. When I see you, I am overjoyed: parts of you like sweetness, a kind eye, a gilded arm. You are the sword in the marsh and not the lady of the lake: water, always water, and I am not a king—I will never be a king despite my name and despite what I have done; firstborn, heaven-sent. You, the second-born are the first gone, and we will remember this, always. You move with the wind.

Where do you go when I cannot see you? How do you breathe in the gold box? How do you breathe in the black pipe? You sprout from the metal like a breath on the air—the image of you before dancing the image I remember: slick-suited, corsaged. You come out when the air is dry and dusty—you, lover of chalk, you, in the hair.

I take a shower to wash the dust from my hair, to rub my eyes without thinking because I will not be needing them where I am going: they will be red as you on the last day, they will be dyed anything other than white, anything other than green. The door will remain closed. The dragon will not snap. I grow taller, my head heavy enough to break my neck, to curl back downward like a sleeping dog, like what was.

Like your name is not your name and you are unchanged. Like your name is within my name; the letters folding in on each other like petals, to let the world know that you are not ready for any of this— the unfolding and the unfurling, rings around rings around rings.

I will pluck you from the circling questions. I will hold you in my palm, crush you with my fingers until you stain my skin orange, until you make my tongue loose in my mouth, until I am changed. I will spit fire until I learn how to throw it like a peach, like something you love, like something you can climb.

SUPER MARIO BROS. 2

Ask me about before. Ask me about the house that was not my
house, the school that was not my school. Ask me about the trees,
how they looked different once, how they changed with the seasons
like tablecloths, like redecorating, like eyes from blue to green and
skin from white to red. Ask me about layering: about putting one
thing on top of the other like a building we have never lived in, like
a door where everything turns to shadow before the sun flares back
out from behind black like a snake, like an extension of ourselves,
like white knuckles. Before, there was a book. Before, there was no
such thing as sleeping, no such thing as subconsciousness, no such
thing as any of that: just pages that we read before bedtime—no, not
before bedtime, this has nothing to do with sleep, this has nothing
to do with any of that. What I remember is what I remember. What
I love is what I love. Please don't remind me of someone. You, with
your slow dig. You, lighter than air if only for a moment. You remind
me of someone I once knew, someone I remember from a dream—red
hair, sharp chin. You remind me of the dark, of pulling grass up from
the earth and hoping for coins, hoping for something that will make
everything except you and I disappear, of hope, of hoping. I want

your face to be your face and no one else's. When you come to me,
arms above your head, please don't remind me of the girl in the book,
don't remind me of the waterfall, don't remind me of long hair and
taking off shoes, the castles made of bones, the way that I replaced
her face with one that smiles when I ask it questions. Here, in the
book that is not a dream, children are missing. This is what happens
when you listen to the words that I am telling you. This is what hap-
pens when the letters form words, form sentences, form something
that reminds you of you, of mud pits and snakes, of floating heads
hungry for a key. Don't ask why we need to go past that door. Don't
ask why it's locked. If you dig a hole, nothing happens. If you dig a
hole, there are people in masks walking between the lines in sand:
they are swallowing mouthfuls. Ask them if they looked different,
once, if their cloaks were pink instead of blue, if their faces were not
masks, if they remember how it was: how they existed, how you are
not dreaming. Wake up. The only way to wake up is to kill the frog.
Before we kill the frog, it is cold. It is cold but we cannot see our
breath: we can walk on the backs of whales and the water will kill us,
freeze us like a body caught in bridge tresses, like being replaced, like
a birthday ride in a hollowed out tree. The trees look different now.
The trees look different now that they have been pulled from their
ground, cut from their branches. Ask me about falling on the ice. Ask
me about the blood pouring from my nose like a silk curtain; ask me
about the other children and their masked faces, their changing eyes.
If I were you, I could float out of here. If I were someone else, I could
jump high enough. If I were someone else, I could dig with my hands
through the snow, through weeks away from dying, through crystal.
Give me a new hat, a red one. Give me a new face, one with eyes that

blink, one where the blood slides right off like my feet on ice. Make me slick. Make me think of nothing but how these hands could touch glass, about how what was once you is now gone, resting comfortably in a book that is not mine, in a book that we would never read before bed, that we would never read to the children before bed in fear that they would wake in the middle of the night and they would find us half naked on the couch reading each other's faces like a dream, like we are trying to remember where we are in the world and why there are no rockets hiding in the ground that can take us someplace a little less cold and a little more like a home that looks like a place we once knew: fountains and wooden tables: a place where there is nothing and nothing missed and everything looks fine. Everything looks as it should be. Everything. Ask me about the frog. Ask me about how we would never put anything in our mouths for fear that we would choke, that an egg would get caught in our mouths. Ask me if I remember you not breathing. Ask me if I remember you out of breath. In our dreams, we can run until we are floating—until our legs hover over the ice like our faces over a sleeping child, until we are frozen without movement. In words, you were never left without breath. In words, we could never run.

SAVE POINT: THE INN

It could have been a number of things. The fear of being in a new country where no one spoke the language apart from a few stunted verbs and a handful of nouns. The cider that started in ceramic bowls but quickly turned to lips around heavy green glassed bottles. The wine we moved toward when we wanted something more familiar and less acidic. But at some point, we decided it was time to steal everything. It could've been the fact that it was dark, it could've been the fact that we were landlocked, whereas the night before we had been on the northern coast of France on the beach, wondering if this was the moment that we would remember, the moment we would bring up at parties when people mentioned the word *night*, the words *when I was younger*. It started small: a loaf of bread from the kitchen that was ripped into smaller pieces and divided amongst us—a clamoring for peanut butter despite nothing resembling what we have known since childhood; we ate it dry to soak up the liquor in our stomachs. We would've eaten anything at this point—anything to take something we know and put it inside us, to warm it in our bellies, to swallow something familiar. We went back for more and came back with more: a dusty bottle of wine—the same wine we drank with dinner by the glass, again, now, we would drink by the bottle; peeling labels, paper from glass, commenting on the glue they use here, how easy it comes off, how simple it would be to poison all of us—to teach us a lesson about kitchens and cupboards, to teach us something valuable about how things are done here, about how instead of waking somewhere new, we would not wake. This happens when we believe that things belong to us—affection after a warm bath, an understanding of what is left of us after we have lost everything. We were brought here to create a longing for something that is not our home: a bed next to a heater, pillows in other languages, a small window to regulate the cold. Food with strange labels, a different type of vegetable rotting in the crisper. To build a city we only know for a second as our own: yes, I remember the train station, yes, I remember the way the ducks walked—their red beaks familiar, conducive to what we believe. This city, too, is ours. We deserve to put it in our pockets: the stream where children threw bicycles, the ring signifying the end, the carnival swirling to greet us the day we arrived. One bottle is certainly enough. One loaf of bread. Any more and they will notice things missing—the count will be off—to steal within sequence. We go back. We go back because it is too warm outside—not yet fall, and our clothes are sticking to our backs, our skin gummed, gritty. We put our bodies in the freezer, we reach our sticky arms into the cold in hopes of something sweet, a dessert, an ending to all things. We have drunk all of the wine. We have drunk all of the wine and we are not sorry—we deserved it, it was there and it was ours. No one will miss it. No one will wonder. Some of us are trying to sleep—some try to ignore what is happening: our beds our alibis. We shout out advice from the floor: walk slower, be quieter, forget about the spoons. We know what will happen: we will wake up in the morning and someone did not throw the empty bottles into the sea. Someone has broken a glass and there is blood everywhere. Someone will walk with a limp. We will return to the ocean from which we once came—a different shore this time.

RAMPAGE

Take the naked woman from the shower and pop her into your
mouth. Chew. Spit her out if she tastes like licorice, if she tastes
like cloth. If you watch what you eat you can live longer. You can
live longer if you watch what you eat. When they jump from the
windows, riding a desk down like a metal dove, like catching a wave
on an ocean that is nowhere near the sour part of this city, close your
eyes and imagine their taste: like flour, like the skin burned off of
a piece of chicken, like a taste you can't get out of your mouth.
Smack your lips like you swallowed a fly, like you were astonished
that anything like this can happen, that buildings can fall down, that
buildings fell. No two alike. When the woman is waving a white
tablecloth out her window as if to surrender, wonder to whom she
is surrendering. Shake the building, watch her fall, watch her walk
to the bottom of the river and resurface like a bobbed apple. It is too
early for apple picking. It is too early for apple picking, so you pluck
fathers by their ties and grind them between your teeth. This one
tastes like chocolate. This one tastes like feathers. Your father worked
on a submarine. Your father flew airplanes, shot rifles. Your father's
eyes, good enough to see you happy, were not good enough to see

other planes. Your father's eyes, good enough to see what all this
means, good enough to see that the man lying on his stomach next
to the left of him, to the right of him, could grow tired of shooting
at cardboard and clay—could turn and shoot him, knock his glasses
off his face. Your father worked in the city in a time when you only
needed to say the name of the floor—the year of my birth. On the day
that no two are alike, think of near misses decades apart, think of rea-
sons to be there: a play, a tour, a restaurant. Think of how he follows
orders: down the stairs of one only to walk up the stairs of the other,
that it's safer in buildings than it is on the ground, that it is easier
to reach down and scoop up than it is to reach across. Your mother
at the plaza. Your mother on the couch. Your mother not painting
ceilings, your mother of what-ifs. Your mother on the other end of
the phone reciting numbers, times, dates, seats. Your mother taking
reservations. Your mother with reservation. The day after. The day
after, a new city: take a nap after all the buildings have been leveled,
after the planes have been plucked from the air, after the stomach-
ache. The day after. The day after, a wedding anniversary: twenty. The
day after, china, platinum. Here, have a coin to remember this day,
but please call heads; call heads every time. Here is a plate, but please
don't eat off this plate—put it on a sturdy shelf, facing outward like
a beacon. Don't use the word *beacon*. Sometimes the windows will
open before I can break the glass. A man is standing there: he wants
to take my picture. He wants to hold what I have left in his hands
like a newspaper, like the head of someone who cannot breathe. I
cannot hold him, can't grasp his body between my swollen fingers
and crush the life out like a daylily. To capture this is to fall, pausing
in midair before sliding down the side of the building like champagne

pouring down a flute. We drank here, once. A toast to this, that, the other thing. This was before my hands were too large to hold a glass. Before, when I was something other than what I am now, something that comes through like a guttural pulse after too many photographs and too little bread. I used to fit inside of these buildings: I used to run my hands against the walls. I used to walk down the hallways with every door open, men in suits and women in red dresses wondering if there were reasons those they loved would be in a city they loved. If I could, I would make a fist around their bodies. I would put them in my mouth to keep them warm.

SHADOWGATE

I was there the day you took everything. I was there the day I taught
you the word for hands, the word for fingers, that the numbers
used to designate the size of rings are less precise: that the metal
will choke your skin like blood lines, like smooth muscles. This was
not that day. This was the day you took everything—a day where
nothing occurred but the unfamiliarity of place—the word *home*
being constructed into something that is not home; far from home,
the word for something left behind. In our new home, everything
sours. In our new home, everything is ours—this pillow as thin as
a door with no keyhole, as thin as a sheet. This hand is ours. These
fingers. This grasp. We hold all things outside of us inside of us on
cards, on black and red things: here is the word *rope* backwards. Here
is something worth remembering. Here is what needs to be said to
become invisible, to pass through locks. We cannot hold these things.
We cannot hold these things, so you took everything: we would hit
people with hammers if we could. We would give them coins that
they do not want; metal that is dull like a glass bottle, like a stale
piece of bread. You put coins into machines that light up like, no,
not Christmas—that day means home, and all we have are hands and

torches. We pay for our curiosity. It is too early in the world for that, too early in the year, too early for cold weather and legs hooked under legs while sleeping. It is too early for all of this. Once, we sat on the beach and watched another country fold in on itself—we could see the lights across the water, and though I hoped they would be green, they were not green. We could see what everything was made from, a slice of the neck, an espionage, a debate over which thing to take and which thing to leave, which thing to open without fear of the ground dropping out from underneath us, which thing to hold onto despite broken legs and broken skulls. Take this book. Take this book and it will be the end of empires. This is what happens when you run your hands over something that does not belong to you. This is what happens when you try to be one with the world. This is what happens when instead of taking my hand, fingers jumping over each other like some ancient game, like a scarf we do not need, you use them to open doors that did not belong to you. Yet this is our house, this is our home—that is our telescope, that is how we know we are here and not there. That is our skull above the door that holds a key to a room that we know. We have memories here: we will always have them, we will never lose them. I am on the floor. I am the floor. I am keeping one eye open. This, certainly, is a trap. This is a trap, it must be, it has to be: someone will appear and hear our whispers, hear the sound of teeth tearing at bread, the sound of a cork leaving glass, the pop it makes. Every step that is not closer to the end is a step closer to the end. We do not bother with glasses: we press the bottle to our lips like it is ours—we do not know where the stemware is, we haven't unpacked anything yet. Our lives in boxes in houses that are not our own and never will be. The day we drank was the day we grew old:

years by seconds, our throats turning to dust before we closed our eyes, before we could blink fast enough. In one minute I will be sixty years older. I will not remember what happened a minute before: it was so long ago. The last thing I remember is standing in front of you while you waved your hands. You are the last in a line of queens. I am the last in a line of kings: where is my wand—it was here when I wrapped it in cloth and made it look like the dead. It was here when I held the torch in my fingers that kept me from the dark and from splitting my head open like a bag of coins. It is dark and there you are, never forgetting. It is dark and you never forget how any of this works, how we exist in this world—to take, take, go to take, go to here. There is no logic—no reason why opening a door would lead to our death, no reason why the ghost who looks like a girl would turn around and smile in our faces while our skin falls from bone like we are stripped of what we have gathered, that this is what our home would be like. The stone walls are uncomfortably close. The stone walls are uncomfortably close, so we think we must move fast: must take, must walk you home. If I stay on the ground, I cannot fall. I cannot make a false move that will cause the candle to hit the ground, to wake the blades, to make a soft spiral lead to red, to have any of this happen. I was there. I was there the day you took everything, and I am on the ground, keeping it all secret. This is that time. This is that time that none of us slept without our stomachs to comfort us, without a bed, without pressing paintings into walls, without the eyes following, without the comfort of seeing ourselves in a mirror unbroken. What you expected hasn't happened. Take the book—fall down. Take the wine, drink it like you have earned it, like it is yours, like you crushed the grapes like a dog's jaw, like there is not a wraith of someone who once lived standing in your way. If we make it, you and I, there will be bread in the morning. We will see crosses, one after another. I will only pretend to look at the stars. I will take some sand from the beach where men I read about were killed. This shell, here, is mine. I will tell myself it was here when the dawn came, when the gates were crashed. There are many strange things in this world. I will tell myself the shell saw it all when it didn't: the animal that lived beneath died only weeks ago, but there is magic here, certainly. I will hold it in my hand like an arrow. You are only more beautiful in the moonlight. I will plunge it deep into your chest until you turn into a wolf. It's a sad thing this has ended.

BOSS BATTLE: A WOMAN MADE OF FEATHERS

When I arrived the music changed—you rotating like a flower with a cracked stem—you rotating like you are caught in the wind: blades on a fan above us where we once slept, a buzz saw, a spinning plate. This is the room you are locked in—deep within a house that someone else has built, rooms leading to other rooms: you in the middle of the eye, you to the east. I remember you beautiful—long-necked, silver-shined, wrists bent in the back of cars, hair on the window. You bit my leg once: drew blood, wiped it on your white coat. If I could fit your body inside my mouth I would, you said, and I believed you: to be swallowed whole like a fish is a noble way to lose one's way—out of breath, crushed to serve a purpose. As you spin your feathers come undone—they crash into the walls, they spin in reverse. I can catch anything you throw at me: grasp it between my fingers; snatch it as it floats to the ground. I try to pluck what is left of you from the air but the vane slices my palm. I will do better. I promise you I will do better. Your feathers get caught in the door. They stick to the walls. Your armor is in the world and you are naked: arms out, palms up. You have lost weight. You have a new bruise, a freckle on your hip I don't remember. I roll my sleeve to my elbow and show you where you bit me: the teeth marks are gone—the skin has snapped back to where it should be. The color, too, is gone: no gradient to red and purple, all anomalies dabbed over. Some of the feathers return to your body; the hollow shaft cuts your skin and digs through the layers of what is left of where you stood, the vane twisting downward. When there are no feathers left the door will open. The music will stop. No one will know we were here.

NINJA GAIDEN

"..."

NINJA GAIDEN II

This is your mission. We begin with silence. We end with silence. I
have told you how it ends: with silence. I have told you how it begins:
with silence. It begins with the repetition of silence, with nothing to
say. Sometimes the eyebrows rise in surprise in silence—sometimes
they loop low like a dead curl, like mountains. We go from a lake to
snow just like that, like nothing was ever worth anything—this is
the street where you grew up. Here is a lock. Here is a lantern. I am
having trouble explaining. Even I don't know for sure. This is your
mission: to shake the dust from bones, to find a face here. If I could
explain to you the patterns, I would let you know that the man with
a mouth for a face will always appear here—the man with a knife for
an arm will always appear here—the spinning brings these things
closer: motion on motion, motion through motion, and this is where
we end with silence. If it sounds like I am talking about nothing, it is
because I am not talking about anything: understanding where there
is no understanding. The girl who shot me in the neck is the same
girl I will marry. I will wear a suit where you can only see my eyes.
I do not know when I was convinced. I do not know when I did the
convincing. In the time between the mine and the snowfall I learned

what your favorite flower is, though I dare not repeat it here. I know your favorite color is green. The song that is playing on loop is your favorite song. It is our song. When the hole in the floor opened and I fell among the pillars you told me all your secrets: the one about the letter, the one about the baby, the one about the cracked smile when the secrets are over. If you turn all of the lights out you will be able to see if you kill all of the bees. You cannot think because the bees are in your head. Ask me a question, you say. Tell me a story, you say. Once upon a time you thought the ashes on my forehead were a bruise. This is where the bees once were. Once upon a time you said that the sky looked like a bruise, that the sky had never been that purple. There is a plan. There is a plan that does not involve me, that there is nothing exact, that there is a new name for things; a year has passed. Don't make me talk about the rooftops. Don't make me talk about the train, about the time that passed, about outrunning. Don't make me talk about what we talked about, about disappearing, about watching the spiders crawl underneath the door into the kitchen, about being bitten in your sleep. Don't make me talk about gatekeeping, about the jumping dogs, about the color green. Don't make me admit I was good. To say that we have done this before is to admit something that we are not ready to admit. After the statues, after the surprise of a gun at our back, we begin again on a train, on top of the buildings we once ran past. It all seems impossible now despite how patient I have become: the comfort in waiting, the love of silence. I am covered except for my eyes that are blue: my eyes are the color of spiders: my eyes are the color of the bag used to haul what is left of the woman who threw herself in front of the train we are sitting in. Don't make me tell you what color I thought the bag would be. Don't make me

repeat myself. You held my hand because there was no other hand to
hold but mine: you are too frightened to touch the window, to touch
the glass where a child put his forehead, to look out at the tresses,
to look down to see if the train was skimming across the water,
freed from its track. Here there is a lot of who are you. There is a
lot of where did you go. The end of your life draws near but I do not
believe it. You ask why anyone would step in front of a train: what
about the family? What about the driver of the train? What about
the passengers forced to ask each other questions about speed versus
skin, about how we pop open, about how easy it is to disappear.
The walls are always moving. There's an altar up ahead somewhere.
You. You're. I've fought this creature before. I can tell you how this
ends—I can tell you where the train ends, where I am always going;
the dreaming of a worst nightmare. You—you are alive. Everyone
who is alive is now alive. There is nothing left to say but each other's
names surrounded by silence. You. You again. You feel like you've
been dreaming for a long time. The part about you and me is true.
Look how beautiful this world is: the trees, the back of buildings. It
will be this beautiful forever. Your name will cling to the walls.

NINJA GAIDEN III

This is your mission. You must understand that this is the end: here is a bird. Here where everything is alone. I killed you? Who is the enemy? What is this place? We are all part of someone's plan—call it what you like. You are my original. I loved you, but not as much as my name.

I'll answer your question: I remember you.

We are still inside the ruins.

1UP

Show me how it is done:

how you add pluses to things,

how you create more than one of anything,

how you are able to sleep at night knowing that if you die the next day you will wake up in your bed as if nothing has happened, how you will see how the day unfold in front of you, like last time, just like the last time.

This time you will not be hit in the face by metal.

This time, you will not take a false step after running too fast and smash your falling body into the side of the ground before falling into some unknown.

At the bottom of the bottomless pit is your bed, yesterday, made by someone who is not you: someone who knows how to use starch, how to make things flat, how to remove stains from the white linens simply by using hot water, who can sew holes up with patches of other lives, can loop weaves and string up and under and over, can pretend like nothing was ever there. Nothing was ever there except the memory of dying the first time and the time before and the time before: the building you run past, the small, scared kitten you jump over.

At the end,
fireworks.

At the end,
the lights turn on.

At the end,
coffee falls from the sky in perfect cups, saucer and all.

At the end, a necklace.

It is either this or it is darkness. It is either this or it is you as a baby again, small yet running as fast as you can because you know what is ahead: what lines to recite, what your bed looks like when you get old enough to sleep alone

old enough to press hands into softness that is not yours,

old enough to push someone away while sleeping.

At some point someone will tell you that you look old for your age, that you are wise beyond your years. You will tell them that monsters are real: you know they are, you just know, you have seen them and there is nothing that mothers and fathers can do to protect you from them. The mothers, the fathers, will say the same thing they always say: turn the lights off. They will hug you and tell you they will keep you safe, that nothing can hurt you.

SIMON'S QUEST

Like all things, we start on a street in front of a church in a town that
we do not know. There are stairs that we must climb and gaps to
be crossed and no sense of direction except we must leave and walk
into the forest. There is no castle here. What we hold is nothing but
an extension of ourselves; we can assume that what is causing fast-
walking bones and rings of light to combust at the slightest touch is
not a weapon but an extension of ourselves; we exist in forms—we
can end others because there is nothing left to hold. When you disap-
pear you leave half a heart, which won't go very far these days. These
days I don't notice when it starts getting dark; the drapes on windows
prevent the sunlight from purely entering my room. These days, there
is a building that blocks my view of the east, the east is home. Across
from my bed is a chair and beyond it a window where the weeds have
grown through the cracks between the glass and the wood, outside
inside if only for a moment. It is too much to go outside during the
day, the sun and the music make things weaker and more susceptible
to the unsurprising fact that the heat causes us to evaporate slowly
toward the clouds. And so this is what heat is like here: we wait for a
time when we have an excuse to do nothing but visit familiar places

over and over, the same gaited walks of friends, the same demons, certainly, and before we know it is night it is night. I am told that it is dark and I am cursed, that my body knows nothing that it knew before. At night, it is difficult for anything to get done, and we know this, that no good comes after the sun goes down, and we must rest, yet we slash at bodies unwilling to yield as they once did. You and you and you and I are old. Things cause more damage after nightfall when our strength has been halved by the process of the day and there is more left to lose, certainly.

This is not a castle—this is a house. This is another house. There are no castles left save for one, which is in ruins. There is the running of ghosts and the breaking of walls. There is nothing to fear here; repeat twice. When you hold certain things you can see things that are not there and this is where we are, in a manor, in a house, in a manner of speaking. You and you and you and I are old—backs are not what they used to be: yours from breaking candelabras in a castle, yours from moving yellow couches from consignment shops to other people's houses in hopes of leaving furniture behind before you leave this place for good; to go to a city where you can talk about this place as if it exists only in theory—that the town gains in magnitude while gone somehow. You say you'll never return unless you are passing through, and I believe and envy your words—that you can leave without fear. I feared the words that scrolled in white and I refused to talk to people, to go up to them and press the button that would make them spell horrible clues, horrible lies and so I paid attention to only the violence—I would jump into pools of water ad nauseam in hopes that I would fall through the water this time, one time, and that repetition

is what get things done most days. In the town next to the town next
to the end, the people tell us to leave, that we have been doing some-
thing wrong all of this time; the obsession of collecting, the trust
we give the ground before falling into spikes. There is something to
be continued, certainly, that the weather can pick us up at any given
moment and bring us to a place where time does not move, day and
night do not cycle, and nothing is protected. If we have enough hearts
we can get what we need to take what is not ours; we must throw
wood into orbs to create something that was once a given, a legend
here that needs no explanation and a hope of leaving ourselves here
so that we can be remembered in all the colors the system allows.
We win, but we are dead. We win, but we cannot bring back what we
have brought back. We win and we are thanked. On the night when I
used to go to church to be healed I heat oil on the stove. I crush garlic
with the broad side of a knife like my grandmother taught me. When
she dies I will leave garlic at the cemetery. When I die I ask that you
leave cinnamon, that these laurels will help me through the poison
that blocks the way to where I am going. We did not think of these
things before today, we did not think about loss, about the acquisi-
tion of the absence of invasion. There is something that needs to be
done, you say. Uncertainty means action and little else. We eat in
silence, this was the appropriate metaphor that I learned as a child,
that I had learned from watching fake sincerity and severity, and this
is what I assumed would happen, that there would be nothing said
except what has already been said, rote memorization and repetition
with no reason to listen again, the text cut short as we jump from
brick to brick in hopes of finding someone willing to sell us some-
thing, exchange what we have for something better, to make a deal.

Brian Oliu

The day we begin to collect the things to put back together in order to destroy the sum of its parts is the day you tell us that they are taking you away from you and I am terrified of what is left to be said and what will be left of me at some point. The second we see where what appears to be ground is not where ground is, we line the path in front of us with prayers and holy water in hopes of seeing the fire at our feet or the sacramental flicker off screen.

ZELDA II: THE ADVENTURE OF LINK

Unlike before we start not in the middle of a decision, not in the middle of the egg, but in a house that someone has built. Unlike before when we were swordless, when we were a child, we have knives, a shield, a weapon to slash out in front of our body like a jabbing tongue, a retracting thorn. We are older now, we are told, we have been tested, we have burned through trees, we have separated rock from rock, evaporated water with a song—here, a pond with no heart—we can only play one song—we can play that song again if we are allowed.

The beauty is that we have lost everything except our sword, except our shield, and there is nothing to remember or to be remembered. We know that it is us only because we are told that it is us; we looked so different then; we can see every stride we make with our legs; we can see our knees bend. Before, we saw ourselves through the eyes of a god, a raven, something we have killed with our sword, turned away with our shield. We used to take the jewels left behind by our enemies and turn them into things that we could hold: a candle, a bottle. Here, now, there is nothing to buy and nothing to take from our slices but experience and the knowledge that we can walk through a place where you once were but are no longer.

We do not know any of this yet. We will touch shadows and be thrown into worlds where we must duck under the emergence of fire from stomachs of creatures we will never be familiar with. We will take lifts and we will be seen. We will turn into fairies for just a few rotations of wings before we fall back toward the grey brick. We will die and we will see a photograph of ourselves multiplied. We will die and someone will lose themselves in the lights. We will die and someone will forget a name they have said before. We will die and someone will put form over function, over meaning, and we will say the word *door* until it looks strange; we will doubt the letters and how it feels in our mouths; nothing can be that round, the door that disappears with a key was never there. We will doubt that someone came in the night and replaced it with something similar while we weren't looking, while we were sleeping. We do not know any of this yet because you are sleeping. We begin when you were sleeping. We begin when you were sleeping and I am sorry. We begin because the end has lost its meaning. We begin because we are meant to believe that after all that transpired between us disappeared, that a birthday passed; that you ate dinner with mothers I will never know; that you are wearing a shirt I have never seen and now you are sleeping. There are stairs to where you are sleeping and I cannot jump up them without jumping through you while you are sleeping. The key to the door is in your mouth but you are sleeping. I will see the fires that surround your bed, my bed I have placed you in while I sleep like a gentleman in a chair close by. I will see the fires that surround my bed. One at your feet, which are bare. One at your hair, which has not moved since August. I will see the fires elsewhere and they will cause me to leap back like a wasp and my body will turn invisible, invincible, and I can run through things that harm me, things that harm you like invisible plans made to cause you to fall asleep elsewhere, all places, but not here. These fires are for decoration; they cannot harm you while you are sleeping.

You do not know this yet, but I will wake up and think you are dead. I will wake up and you will be dead and you will not wake up. I will wake up and I will be dead and you will not wake up. I will be dead and you will wake up and you will get a drink of water and look in the mirror and I will be dead. I will be dead and you will wake up and you will kiss me on the forehead and I will kiss you on the forehead and I will be asleep. I will be dead and you will walk through a door and then another door and you will leave and I will be dead and you will play a song like a boat on an ocean, like a night moth, like a sad bird and I will reflect in the keys like a Spanish melody, like a shadow that I have been carrying that spills out from my stomach when the lights go out and the courage is lost. I will kneel in the corner and stab at the air until my shadow walks into me—jumps with knife pointed downward to the earth, and you will be asleep. I will sleep on the floor on my side like a wound, like the taste of grapes.

We were in love until we reached the end.

CONTRA

In your first life, you were foolish—running where you shouldn't run, crashing into trees, touching everything you saw. In your next life, you were more cautious—ducking when things were thrown your way, jumping over crevasses. In your next life, the sky started to fall in—talons of birds you have never seen in any of your lives. In the lives after that, you began to understand the world you were placed in: that things, terrible things, can come at you from behind, from underneath. To be swept off one's feet only to fall again from the sky, curled up in a ball, rotating. When I saw you, surrounded, you were aware of the names of things—you knew that when you jumped you could move back and forth in mid-air like a balloon, like wings, like spiraling. You knew what things to touch—wings that fell from the sky like you once did after the sixteenth time that you died, wings that would make you stronger—wings that allowed you to remove self from self, to streak ahead of your body like a flashlight, turning all things white. In this life, you do not know the world we live in. You do not know how quickly the seasons change, how fast it can go from leaves as thick as bulbs, from snakes moving with a quickness, from mosquitoes biting your white legs while we sit in the backyard.

You look like the type that smokes cigarettes: you will not let me light it for you. In a past life, you would have let me come closer, would have let me bring my hand as close to your mouth as possible without touching it, allowing you to breathe on my hand before snapping your neck upward and exhaling. You are always looking up. You are always pressing your chin to your chest while you walk, as if you can see through the ground that we walk on, as if there is something in the water. There is always something in the water: there is nothing I can do about this. Believe me when I say that I am the only one: I do not control the fire. I do not control the mouths on doors, the sickles. Yet you blame me for it. You blame me for being here: for the roaches that try to crawl into your ears while you sleep, that cause you to forget how to exhale, how to breathe on my hand. You heard a story about their white blood, about living on without a head, about how they will run to your hands if you have been cutting onions for soup. Do not worry about these things. Do not worry about your eyelashes being eaten while you sleep. Do not worry about the rat that lived beneath my crib when I was a child, about how it would scale the bedpost like you climb up to where the water falls. These are things to worry about elsewhere. These worries are for future lives. You, in your new life, have no time to rest. Rest is a number. Talking is a number. This has nothing to do with change, with having to get to work, with throwing an onion at your back. I do not know that if you have time to sit down: to have a meal, to talk about things—the world you are trying to save, the people you are trying to defend. I am scared to touch your hand for fear that you might die. I am scared to make a noise for fear that I might die. When you leave here, you will step incorrectly. You will fall from the sky like you always do. You will start running forward. You will restart where you fell, circling—the yard, the kitchen. You will keep going and you will remember none of this—how you got out of this building, why you arrived, why all of the roaches are dead, why it is snowing, why we are wearing white. If you remembered me, you would remember me as faceless. You would remember my motions—where I came from, when I jumped, what patterns I made. You would remember that you cannot touch me without falling to the ground. I would tell you that to touch my skin is worth dying a twenty-third time, a twenty-fourth, a twenty-fifth. This is what I was running toward you to tell you. This is why you laid me to waste.

BALLOON FIGHT

I wake up and it is dark. Outside, too, it is dark, but there is no way
of knowing. How anyone can see at night is a mystery—it is dark
and it is important to see my palm, to see the lines, to see the folds
between rows of horizons like roads, like the skyline. I can't tell you
about the day I couldn't see. I can't tell you what was written there:
what day it was. I woke up and it was dark and it was Tuesday. I did
not see this written anywhere. Read to me: tell me what these letters
are, what words they will never form. Tell me about the curve in the
C, the line of the Z. There is an apple. Where is the apple: on the
table, on the ground, in the air. Someone has thrown the apple across
the table. It bounced off of my chest like a bluebird hitting a window.
There is no way to see this coming. I have never seen an apple float.
The apple is on the table: it must be on the table or the deer will eat
it. I never saw the deer. I only saw the hole it left in the apple, the
hole it left in the grille of my mother's car. My mother does not see
well at night. My mother does not drive on that road anymore. A girl
asked me if I liked her blue dress. I told her it was green. I should
have never believed her.

If you look into my eyes you can see a soft ring of blue where the white should be. If you look into my eyes you won't see anything else—this is my promise to you. A boy at my birthday party had his eye poked with a zipper. I did not understand how this could happen: a boy, a zipper, a birthday, an eye. Some things are not meant to be opened. We all wanted to lift up the blue patch over his right eye, to see what was under there, to understand why it needed protection from candlelight. If we lifted up the plastic, he said, his eye would fall out and roll across the floor into the kitchen where the man was making dinner. In the mirror, I watch an eyelash slide behind my eye. I wonder what is back there.

If you look close you can see the knife, the fork. Here you are. Here is the eye. Here is the eyelash. You cannot see it though it is in front of you. That is your eye in the mirror. That is the balloon on your back. There is the hook on the ground that you will step on: it will be dark. You could never see the ground in front of you: you are walking on air, always. They will scrape the rust from your skin like peeling an apple. There is fur and blood in the metal. The tissue will feather. Your eyes will be closed.

I wake up and it is dark. If I blink, I will see worms in the air, all of their parts separated like a shelf of books, like slices of pie. I liked to crush caterpillars into the carpet, to watch them curl into swirls, into rings. When they died, they would smell like the closet where we hid suitcases, where I would sit in the dark and try to see my fingers in front of me, to try to read the letters on my shirt. I try to catch the worms but they float like balloons, like apples with bite wounds, like a deer dead on impact. At the end of the road a balloon will appear, and I wait for it to come into focus, to float over the tree lines and electrical wires. They ask if I know what a balloon looks like, and I say yes, that I like the red ones. I tell them about the time I dreamt I was in a hot-air balloon. The children in the park waved as I took off. I kept rising until it was night—the flame from the burner the only thing I could see. I grew old in the basket—the hand in front of my face spotted with age. The children had long since stopped waving.

BOSS BATTLE: THE EYE FROM WHICH WE SEE OURSELVES

When I arrived, the music changed—the perspective changed as well: from what I see to what you see, eyes behind glass, frames of black where I would hide if I could make myself flat as a coin on the ground, so thin you couldn't grab my body with wet fingers. Instead of standing before me, taller than I remember, you are a ghost who sees everything—you move as I move, you follow my actions, the search for something to hit, the right temperature to set something on fire. Of the things I have forgotten to mention, this is one: it is dark in here and you are the only thing that can see—I see myself how you see me, green like a waxy leaf, maybe, green like crawling.

I have never told you this, but how you see me is how I see myself— the back of my head, the collar stretched to hide blemishes on my neck, my shoulders broader than they were when I was learning how to lift: the bottle I needed two arms to carry can be lifted with fingers, with the wrapping of palms. Tell me this story: say it to me in my voice, lower than yours. I have never heard you speak—a simple word will do: *someone, circle, window*, something to let me know that you are thinking of these things instead of watching all that I do and all that I don't. That when there are cracks in the screen like wasp nests, you will carry me over felt lines until someone, anyone, can see where I am going.

DONKEY KONG

Start with the neck. Wait. Before you start with the neck, start with
a shirt, a belt, a pair of trousers. Start with the feet. These shoes are
old. These shoes do not fit—the leather on the back scrapes your
heels. It leaves a line like the one on the wrist of a girl you think
about often. You think about her often, but think of the raised red
skin. Start with the wrist. You don't wear a watch. You don't know
what time it is. You are seventeen minutes late to everything: the girl
you think about often tells you this. Five means twenty-two. The day
you were supposed to start with the neck you were running late—you
had been sleeping. Start three days ago. Start with an old t-shirt and
gym shorts. Start with missing. Start with not being dressed for the
occasion. Start with that. Start with not having the time to say good-
bye. Start a year ago: start with white shirts with no collars. Start
years ago. Start saying goodbye years ago: gaps in the architecture,
boiling water for coffee when there is coffee on the table. Here is a
pair of trousers. Put the left leg in. Put the right leg in. Understand
that there are ladders that you cannot climb—there are rungs
missing. Wrap the belt around your waist like a tongue. Push the
metal clasp through the hole and tighten. Make it press against your

stomach: you were not meant for clothes. Later, slap at the leather like an oaf, like an ape. You do not deserve to wear anything, especially today. These are not the tools you know how to use. There is a hammer floating here—you do not know what it does. You cannot fix the holes. You cannot climb the ladder. You are afraid of heights. You are afraid of climbing. Start there. Start with the shirt—think about the ones he wore when we knew he was dying. Think of the shirts we bought for him then. This is the shirt you sleep in. This is the shirt no one sees. Start buttoning. Start with the neck. No. Start with the bottom: run your hands over the two circles with no matches. This is excess. Smell the starch. They will not let you in the church if your shirt is wrinkled. They will not let you mourn. They will not let you put your hand on your father's shoulder as he stands over the casket. They will not let you remove a piece of string from his sport coat. Here is a tie. Rest it on the back of your neck like a snake. Look in the mirror. Follow your hands: the thick end over the thin end, one side shorter than the other. Do it wrong. Start again. Here is a tie. Rest it on the back of your neck like you are carrying someone. Don't pay attention to your hands: one end over the other. Cross over. Cross under. Do it wrong. Ask your father on the day of his father's funeral to tie it for you. Apologize. Apologize again. Say nothing when he says you need to learn how to do this yourself. Know that he is right. Apologize again. Take the noose and put it over your head. You should be wearing a bib. You are a child. You are a baby. If you cannot peel a banana how can you dress yourself. You should've started over. You should've started with the button at the top of the dress shirt. Started thumbing at the circle, the eye slit in the fabric where it belongs, where it should lock into place. Started there. The cloth should press into your throat—it will move the hairs left from not shaving close enough, it will turn your skin red. A little girl will touch your face and ask you if you have a mother. You will say yes, and she will think you mean your wife. You do not have a wife, you say, and she says you must: your cheeks are rough. You must be married. You must have a child—maybe even younger than herself. You will tell her no, you have none of these things, and she will be disappointed. She will not believe you. Pull the knot toward your chin and watch the tie lengthen.

GOONIES II

A confession: I do not know where I am going. Some days, while I walk through doors that slam behind me like the opening of wings, my perspective changes—instead of watching me mark time with my back toward you and my eyes toward another, I am facing you—my eyes pink and hopeful like a baby mouse, like a tongue—my body swinging toward you but not moving—left arm up, right arm up, left, right. There was that time, outside this house, we made a bridge to cross—we put down rocks and mud to stop the creek from flowing: to end gravity, to halt the natural movement of things. Welcome here. You are welcome here. Are you tired? Are you tired from digging, from believing you can change the layout of the ground—that you can pick up gravel into your hands and throw it into the air like it is confetti: like there is a parade and you are invited, like the rocks would float down from the sky like bats, like skulls with no neck bones, like jaws. That everyone would laugh: that you could throw the rocks higher than anyone, that they would snap back to your hand if you asked them—a videotape in reverse—the luckiest catch in the world. That you could swing a hammer: that it would connect somewhere—a nose, an eye, an arm, and there would be no consequence—that there would be no blood rushing out of mouths, that they wouldn't be frightened, that they would allow you to rest here; that you could close your eyes and feel new—can see without glasses, can breathe underwater. If you believe that, that you can punch a wall while locked in your room and make something appear other than fear and heat between your knuckles, then you can believe that there is something to all this—that there are rivers that stop, that there are bridges, leaves, wood. That you are two minutes late. That I felt you here. That there are rivers that flow backwards: that the water snaps back into my hand like a ball on a string. I do not know where I am going and my hands are dirty. Our hands are dirty and it is getting dark. There are mice out here, certainly, and we have forgotten our way back to where you live, to where your parents are waiting for us, to where there were not enough people in our lives to pretend some were missing.

I planned for this. There is no way you will believe me, but I promise you I did. I know where we were—we were in the attic because there were rats there: fat bodies with long tails that coiled around your wrist like a bracelet, like a rubber band reminding you of something, someone—a reminder you have been here before, a reminder there are people missing. A reminder you are missed. There were places where we could walk—slats of wood the width of your foot after it has swollen up like something bit it: small insects making you larger than you can imagine, your skin expanding like a loaf of bread, like the length of the word *pink* on your tongue, like a bruise, like all those things. This is what happens when things go wrong. You're late. I was almost killed. Be careful where you step or you will fall through the ceiling of a white room made of white bricks the color of a string—of the twisted rope that kept the spinning orb elevated, of the string that pressed into your finger as if to leave a gap where a ring should be, as if I were married, as if this is hush-hush. When I was a child, there were rats in my house. They would sleep underneath my bed. I would imagine their teeth next to my cheek, their nose against my nose. I saw one once—a long tube of hair snug between two pieces of wood: eyes closed, mouth open. This is how you will find me: in the woods, in the bridge I tried to make, in the river. I put myself into the world—I swung a fist and hit the ground—my hands are dirty. Please help me: what do you do. This is where it all changes. This is where it all turns back. Do not do this—any of this. No one will forgive you. You will not be welcome. Get out of here if you have nothing to do. You will not be welcome.

BOSS BATTLE: THE THING THAT BURROWS UP TO GREET US

When I arrived the music changed—a descending scale, a trickle down as if someone was pulling a string through my ear. Think of how light I must be, for once. Think of how the sand keeps me upright instead of pushing me downward to something we cannot see through: that the room is filled with silt and yet the hair on top of our heads is not brushing against the ceiling, that before the wind blew the dust through the doors this place was larger than my heart gave it credit for; air above our bodies for miles, our knuckles will not scrape against the plaster if we raise our fists to fight or if we raise our hands to surrender. I don't remember my legs becoming heavy, the sand up to my knees. I don't remember anything gradual about this, anything granular: a slight incline, an ache in my calves. All I know is you are digging and I am not. You resurface from the ground like a chubby arm outstretched past the breakers. All I can do is wait. I cannot dig and so I must wait. You are gone and I must wait for you to return so I can strike between your eyes, so I can send you somewhere you won't resurface. I wish that instead of you putting yourself underground it was something else entirely, that you don't have the right to appear on cold nights or long nights or nights where I should be anywhere else but right here. I can mount you on the wall and shut the door behind me. Instead there is sand in my mouth and sand in my heart. Instead, my feet are wet from the rain and the sand sticks to my skin.

DRAGON WARRIOR

I go then you go then I wait. Little is known about anything except the ancestry that exists only in exposition, in rumors spit forth in white text by old men who all look the same. The knights, they look the same as well, but their eyes are kinder now than before; grey lines on fat faces looking east, west, instead of south, always south. Once we are finished something will be revealed other than my name, shortened by restraints in characters and character, a name rendered obsolete. I go and then you go then I go then you run. At the end of things I am asked a question that I answer incorrectly and I am killed. The colors change when I am about to die and they change when I am dead. You talk to me about leaves. You talk to me about how beautiful it is when they die. You send me a letter in the mail with dead leaves and you ask me if I miss the colors and I say yes and this is all I say. You say that you have been waiting a long time for this time to arrive and for me to arrive. I can rule half the world, you say, and I say yes. You tell me about death as quickly as possible and tell me that my deeds to date will not be lost in the shuffle of what should be a simple algorithm, that there is nothing between us but admiration and water that cannot be marked by a cartographer's hand—hic sunt dracones—hic sunt leones; in these places elephants are born, in these places scorpions are born, here, dog-headed beings are born, and I have seen these monsters appear out of air like November, and I have moved from one square to another to see these things—no movements diagonal, all movements like the sign of the cross, eliminated here, and I have been asked for a command. Here, lions abound. Here, terra pericolosa. Here, I will walk, accosted by things I must kill, things I must gather to acquire the experience to say the words to sleep, to say the words to hurt, to say the words to hurt more. Your ears burn when you are talked about and when you are poisoned. Fortune smiles upon me and I say yes. You tell me that my journey is over. You tell me that I must take now a long, long, rest and the colors change and the trees do not move. The water does not move. It was kind of you to save everything that I have done before you put an end to everything; to place all that I have learned in boxes and nonvolatile storage—a photograph, some text. In the past, I would sleep at the church. In the past, I would sleep at the inn. I would sleep in the castle where the king stood. I will sleep here. I will not wake up until I leave this world and reset everything with fingers, with bones on top of bones like lighthouses, like whatever is left before this idea of permanent death, this foreign concept of nothing left. I return as if nothing has ever happened and you will ask the same questions about the leaves and what is left of this place, what remains on the ground. I built a bridge to get here. Someone built a bridge to get here. I say no and you go then I go then you heal then I wait. I go then you go and I run but cannot and you go and I go and then you go then I heal then you go. This is how it works now. You are indefinite—you are a lord, a keeper of bread. You are never the lord, the keeper of bread, the keeper of all things, the end the end an end. You are defeated and you are a dragon and you are here and I am here. I heal and you go and I heal and you go and I heal more and you go. I have done well in defeating. All shadows are banished, peace is restored, and I am carrying you, somehow through the swamp, through the mountains. There is nothing here but you. Here be you. The king offers me the crown and I have no choice in the matter. I speak in words. I will leave but you know the word *stairs*. You ask if you can travel as my companion. No. But you must. You ask if you can travel as my companion. No. But you must. You ask if you can travel as my companion. Yes. You are happy. The knights' swords turn to trumpets and play a song. This will inspire a ballet once we are through with everything; a child in red shoes will run across a stage and bow and we will clap. You are wearing makeup and you are beautiful. Once we are through with everything I will pick the pieces of metal that keep your hair in place from your scalp like ashes, like scales, like leaves. I will set them on a table. You cannot sleep with your hair like this; you will be stabbed in your sleep.

PUNCH-OUT!!

Come in close and I will teach you a lesson. You will fall down. He will swing—shoulder to arm to hand, and it will strike you on the cheek. Your head will spin backward like the hair of the woman in the second row. Get up. He will blink. His eye might sparkle. He might open his mouth. He might flicker once—his body will disappear and reset, ready to cause damage. If you jump high enough you can hit him in the chin. Punch until you turn pink. You are medicine. You are without heart. When you get older, you will punch less. You thought you were still a teenager. When you get older, you will see all of this coming—the wind up, the drop of the left before the right enters your body, the face, always the face. I am a beautiful fighter. I have such a style. I will picture my fist breaking through the back of your skull. I will have hair on my arm. I want to touch the space behind the space where you stand. Tell me you understand what this means. Tell me there is something to this. I have a weakness but I will not tell you. Someone threw a piece of candy into the ring. Someone had his nose broken. This fighter has been looking forward to this for months. After you lose, we'll drink to your health. The boy with a broken jaw has a broken jaw. This is what he'll tell his mother: he'll say that he

forgot something. I am sorry you have to see me like this. Thank you
for seeing me like this—I didn't mean to be a bother—thank you for
seeing me. Think of the time I walked you to the train. Think of how
poorly the visit went, my knuckles clumsy. I do not remember where
I slept. I think you're going to have a nightmare tonight. Someone
beautiful and small wants nothing to do with you. Someone beautiful
and small wants everything to do with you. Someone beautiful and
small wants to kill you, to punch his way through your stomach, to
walk away, retire. I am tired of talking. In the morning, after dropping
you off, men staggered into the courtyard and wanted to fight me.
Their threats started in a language that was not my own, and gradu-
ated into words that I could parcel out, words that would cause me
to leave a man bloodied. They tried to kick me, and I laughed: a fist is
the same in any language. I would say that I ran back home without
you as the sun rose, but it was still dark by the time I crawled into
my bed. I hid my hand underneath the pillow to cool it down from
the heat caused by swinging it like a king, like a champion. It is
not because I didn't want to look at the hand that formed the fist
that hurt the man. I am proud of this, you know. I made someone I
had never met understand. I would have punched myself out. I would
have turned purple. I ruined your night, and it is beautiful. The first
one, definitely, was beautiful. The second, definitely, was not. It was
as sloppy as my tongue attempting words to get you to leave. I did
not know the word for stop. I did not know the word for leave me
alone, I have left a girl who will never love me at a train station so
she can catch an early flight back to hands that will hold her and ears
that will smile when she mentions how strange everything was. It
was a beautiful country, she will tell them, and they'll nod. She will

show them pictures and I will not be in any frame. They will ask why she went and she will not be able to explain anything further than a name. She will not be able to explain in any language why we will never talk again. I did not know the words for this so I broke your fucking nose. I yell that I broke your fucking nose in my words, not yours. I do not bother with your language. My punch is soft like your heart. I'll be trash and I'll be scum, but I'll be angelic trash and scum. When I woke up in the afternoon, my pillow was red. My sheets were red too. I threw them in my suitcase and rolled it over cobblestones to the laundromat. When I opened the gates no one was waiting for me. I poured the powdered soap into the machine. I would say I watched the fabric spin and my blood disappear, but I read a book. I would say I watched the fabric spin and you disappear, your scent, your hair, but I thumbed at the scrapes on my hand instead—my blood had turned to paper.

SUPER MARIO BROS. 3

I heard you can fly. I heard you can throw fire. You can throw fire, but you've always been able to do that; you can change colors at the touch of a flower, you can crush a petal in your palm, you can cause a reaction by shaking your fist. You've always been able to do this. You will always be able to do this. I heard you can fly. We do not care about percussion. We do not care about compression. We heard you can fly. The first time I died, the ground dropped out from underneath my feet because you did not teach me how to fly. I heard that my mother's eyes wouldn't stop watering. The carpet below our shoes was white. The tile in the kitchen was white. We heard about a woman who tried to fly around the world and went missing. We will repeat this message. We heard about a woman who tried to fly around the world and went missing. We will repeat this on 6210 kilocycles. Wait. In all her glory, my mother's eyes are watering. Wait. We heard about an anchor. We heard the ship cannot move if you have an anchor. Inside of a white house inside of my chest is an anchor. If you die, the ship will not move. Your children are trying to kill me. The verb *to plead* has changed its meaning. You are crushed with a silence, with a flute sounding upward like a bird, like a soprano. All things are in musth periodically—to understand what it is to be a man, to understand what is left after weight crushes weight, the sound of nothing except a neck sliding within a shell, and I am sorry that your kingdom does not exist in this castle, and I am sorry that as I hold onto what I am told is dear to me, the floor drops out—this room turns to clouds and I am falling, bodies hitting the carpets of kings like a leg hitting water, I heard that if your timing were right, you would not die. You can hold onto these things: that there is nothing to worry about, that the ghosts will not follow if you look them in the eye. You appear only after everything is well taken care of, all of the stars collected in my pocket like a stopwatch, like time standing still. I am sitting on the floor in a place where women try on dresses. I can see the feet of others—the painted toenails I would see only in shoes, the stockings colored like skin—but I was caught up in words. I heard there is a place where everything you know is larger. There is no explanation. I heard that if you knelt in a place long enough you would fall through the floor to the ground; that you would hide in the background, that you could run behind darkness until something appeared. This is not how it works. There is a child that knows how to do this without any knowledge of colors or how this world works. I am not him. I need to leave this place where I can walk behind things I have always walked in front of; that there is something to the way that my arms jut out from sides when running, that we are a plane, that we are setting the table. My arm hangs to the side of my body like a bag of dead leaves. I keep my hand in my pocket when I walk. I do not punch questions because I have memorized the answers. I know all of the movements. One year my cousin dressed up like the woman in the airship. I used to pour buckets of water on her head and she would cry that she was drowning. I have heard that if you wait, all things are possible. I heard you had a twin sister that drowned in the ocean. I heard that you got married and she ate the wedding whole. I heard that she was dead two years after she died. I heard she lived in a castle. I heard that if you can fly forever then you can fly forever. I would've flown forever if I were you. If I were you, I would've jumped earlier. I would've taken all of the memories and placed them in a stomach in a desert some place. I would've broken a rock with a hammer. I would've swum under the ship. I would've done a lot of things.

BOSS BATTLE: THE GOLD ROBOT

When I arrived, the music changed—cut clean like a glinting tooth, a silence that weighed, a full stop. You on your side like a stomachache, like a sick dog. I can imagine you young, freshly assembled, your body larger than the room you were built in. When you creaked to, you punched the sky and shook the walls. Whoever made you did not understand the meaning of anything: the hum of lips like helicopter blades chopping at the wind, the slight buzz that you feel right between the eyes as the machine warms. The boast and bravado, the ultimate creation, the eight times my size seems silly now in your stillness—we fight through smaller versions of you to get to you: children with sawblades for hands, spring coils for feet. The cuts on my arms, the burnt skin from hot metal, the smooth charred ends of shocked fingers mean nothing if there is no one to show them to: you, bulbs smoked out, teeth rusted, should be surprised that I made it this far, that you are impressed with my character, that it is too bad my journey ends here. I can imagine our battle—long with rising frustration, steam from our ears, each swing a question on the air, asking if there will be damage this time, a flipped switch, a slow dance, an experiment in what it means to be broken and what it means to break. Instead you are a nothing with no lights, a closed file, a peaceful end.

GRADIUS

What you have heard is true: we are falling in grades into the river.
The gazebo will go first—its base will be unearthed and it will topple
into the water like a coffee urn, like a groomsman at the reception.
This architecture floats. This pavilion is an object of pleasure. The
pagoda floats—the belvedere is lovely. The gazebo in the river has
many names: how beautiful, how I shall gaze. The floors are uneven
and what you heard is true. Here: stand here. Now stand here: you
are shorter now. They pressed your plastic feet into the icing of the
cake—the bottom of your dress lined with a ring of white icing.
Please do not lick the bottom of your flattened feet—do not dab at
the skirt with your thumb.

What you have heard is true: there is nothing left here but salaman-
ders and movement. There is the sight of wind if you could see wind,
if you could see it sprawling out from our backs like tails, like turning
your head too fast, like too much perfume. Above the cats and above
the library and above the folly is an airplane spewing smoke as it
crashes: an airplane with a banner trailing its body. It is telling you
and me to eat something, it is telling us to call someone. All of the

letters and numbers are reversed: here is an eight, here is a zero, here is a child's S curled like a lizard, unraveled like a snake. I am watching you watch the water roll in and it is beautiful—you with the beginnings of a freckle and me with beginnings of little to be proud of, sand not yet made into castles, places to live, a gazebo, an elsewhere. In the airplane is a man who does not know about these things—a man who sees horizons from anywhere but through glass: a plastic tree, a hollowed rock. Here is where we put the water in.

In the airplane there are lights. We know this. We know this but choose not to look at what is left—there is something here; there is something here too. We choose not to leave. We imagine being in a body inside of an airplane inside of a body—his body perhaps, watching his blood drift toward us, white and red cells, walls of stomach, a kidney here, romance and remembrance of the things inside eyes, what has been seen. We see things floating like orphans, like our brain reaching out to touch us, like an impossible wall. What you have heard is true: this happens when you stare at too much blue or too much white or too much you—it all dances—snakes and liars, centipedes and rotting logs, hellbenders from torrents and sirens, viruses maybe, with their fat heads and little legs lumbering slowly like a child, like us when we were children, looking up at the sky like a lost limb at night or like me and you on an evening we went east only to sit, nothing left but sitting—not moving—our blood the temperature of water: stylish and lungless. What you have heard is true: we do not follow the lights. I asked what we were looking for. I asked what we were looking for and you said nothing. Your body is leaving you. There is a chip there, there is a vessel—there is something

inside you that causes you to take your hair out piece by piece, to
leave patterns on your scalp, to pluck your eyebrows out of your face,
to take your eyelashes and hold them between your freckled fingers
and blow them out onto the river that has become the sea, to make a
wish you say, you tell me to make a wish, make a wish, you say, make
a wish you say again, make a wish for each punctuation mark, each
comma, apostrophe, pause, possession, make a wish because they
always grow back—these pieces of self lost in the red clay that is left,
we cannot make wishes while they are still attached to our bodies,
we must speed up, we must double our wishes, we must double our
options. I wish I could say a part of you floated in the air toward the
propeller: a ceiling fan moving forward. I wish I could tell you these
things, I wish what you have heard was true, that you are beautiful
bald, that there are reasons for anything beyond living, that each
piece of hair is actually something to hold onto after it has become
detached from what you are and what is left. There is nothing here
but rocks, you say, and nothing could be further from the truth—
here is a pulse, here is a piece of glass. They will make statues of us
from these rocks, I say. Our ears will be pressed to the ground. Our
mouths will be open.

KID ICARUS

This is where I try to remember. This is where I try to remember
what has happened before this, any of this: where you were, where
it started. It started at the bottom, with water everywhere. I know
the weather everywhere. I turned off the lights. I turned off the lights
because we are too far from the sun and there was something else.
There was. This is what has happened. Forget that. This is what will
happen. There will be wings that don't work: they will pierce my
skin and hang from my shoulders like a dead plant. I do not believe
that they are made of wax—I do not believe they will melt. At the
top there is a prison, you say, and I agree: you are the holder of light,
you have tended the garden. You think I am an angel. You think I am
not a man: that I can move among the waves and not lose anything.
You think that I can fly. Tell me the story again. Tell me the story of
where you met me and how you knew how I slept like a child with
my knees pulled up to my chest. Tell me the story of how you knew
I stuck an arrow in my mouth and swallowed: the wood piercing
my throat and how I kept the water running to cover the sound of
my coughing. Tell me what I said it tasted like. Tell me about the
dead trees whose branches look like smoke moving west. Tell me

that you're glad I came—to save you from rotting columns and wax candles. I am named after a void: a gap in the floor that I create as I move closer to where you are. I hear that you are having a baby. I hear that the lines in your face make you look older: a few coats of silver where black should be. Remember how I jump. Remember how I can make myself better—the arrows shoot farther than before—they linger in the air before disappearing into the dark, the sharp head dulling to nothing as it vanishes before it strikes your eye. You think you are rescuing me from all of this: you have given me a bow to escape here, to pretend the heat and the sticking of skin to sheets is something that can be plucked out like the strings on a harp or a snake out of the riverbed. I will believe that I can be saved: that the rings around my wrist can rotate around me like I am a god and you are a goddess—that there is light here, that there is water to drink that does not come from the river. We will not feel the grit of silt on our teeth. These wings will not work. They are not like bird limbs. I will not lift. I will not drag. I will not glide the way that you want me to: like a mute swan, like I am ruby-throated. I can adapt, you say. It has nothing to do with angels and everything to do with angles: here are the numbers, here is how you ascend. Think of silk. My bones are made of palms: bend them into a cross. Comment on my shape—a diamond, a triangle, the top of the umbrella you left in my closet. Tie a knot around my stomach. You believe I am the lightest. You believe that I am made of silk: that whatever weight is left is less than the air, that at the end of all of this I can be more than what I am—I can double in size like you wished it to happen—that nothing needs to be said: you, standing in front of me after I killed the girl in the eye. You behind the eye. You in front of a mirror, waving, you standing there all of this time as if you were a statue, a marble pillar, as if you knew that we were starting in the middle, as if I was not the last hope but just a hope—an attempt, a try. You running, trying to catch the wind. Move with me and I will move—I will move like there is nothing left. I will move like a myth on the air, like rocks falling from the sky. I will move like there is nothing worth remembering.

R.B.I. BASEBALL

This is the part where we are supposed to keep an eye on things.
This is the part where our eye will not move, will not dart to some-
thing else flickering: the sight of something white waving, the shape
of mouths forming words that are lost in the lights. My right eye
twitches when I have had too little sleep. It twitches when I can't
think of words to say—skin spitting words in the form of waves, a
ball fluttering above the white plate before diving into the dirt. There
is a belief that if you can see something then you can hit it—strike
it out of the air like a gnat circling—to smack a body with a palm,
to have it change directions suddenly. I will stand, shoulders cocked
back like I am trying to push my bones up through my skin—like I am
trying to spread wings—like I am trying to understand flight. Swing,
you say, and I do: I hit nothing but air and myself—the barrel of metal
slapping my back on the follow-through like I was meant to do that:
like I was being celebrated, like I had earned the right to shake hands,
to smoke cigars, to kiss the girl who wore red. Keep an eye on none
of those things. Do not look at any of those things—do not picture
them in your head, do not place their faces in the stitching. When
you make contact, when you hear metal hit leather: run. Your mother,

there, will blink. Your father, there too, will blink. I cannot hear what
they are saying. I cannot hear what they are saying but it sounds like
static, like white noise, like the cat pawing at the pond behind our
house, like water slurring. If I could see their mouths then I could see
what they were saying: about neglect, about a car shifting from park
to neutral, about the tire running over my leg like a dead rabbit, like
a lump of skin in the middle of the road. I cannot see their mouths
because I need to keep my eye on the ball. My eye is on the ball and
it is getting closer. My eye is on the ball and it is getting closer and
the mouths are getting larger: hands over faces like whispers, like I
am stealing signs, like I am reading lips. He is going to do this. He is
going to do this and then that. They will never tell: inside, outside,
fast, slow. This is the part where I am supposed to keep an eye on
things. This is the part where I am supposed to keep an eye on things
but it is closing up without asking, quivering. This is where I wonder.
This is where the ball hits me square on the back. This is where I
make contact: run. This is what I practiced for. This is where I re-
member tossing the ball up in the air and swinging. This is where I
missed the ball. This is where I missed the ball and hit you—the bone
above your eye the sweetest spot. This is where I bring you into the
house from the yard and explain to your father what happened, it was
an accident, I did not mean to make contact, I never make contact, I
can be trusted. I promise I can be trusted. Trust me, I can be trusted.
If I meant to do it I would have hit him behind the eyes. I would have
hit him behind the eyes and he would have dropped like a stone, like
a dead fir root, like a sack of bones. The next day, the children asked
what happened and you pointed at me; you said it was on purpose,
that it was with purpose. You said I kept my eye on it. You said I kept

my eye on your eye and I swung through it—I can hit anything I want to. I have such accuracy. I can hit flares and bombs and frozen ropes. I can hit the barn. I can hit the world. The children will have nothing to do with this. The children believe in justice. The children put a grocery bag over my head and punched me through it, their small fists hitting neck and cheek. Keep your eye on the darkness—do not listen to what they are saying: their words are hollow—rhubarb, peas and carrots, watermelon, wallow, wallow, wallow. How much longer. How much longer. How much longer.

If you could see me out there, you could see me swatting the flies above my head, the flowers in the field. If I had the time I would steal one from the ground, separate earth from taproot and place it behind my ear like a pencil, a reminder of where I am and what I can do. If I had the time, I would take a breath and blow florets—I would scatter the whiteness on the wind, I would make things grow: a milk pot of dog's milk, a monk's crown, a mole's salad. If I had the time, I would snap the stem with a quiet crack, I would hold the yellow flower under my chin and ask you if I like butter—if I would slide it into small squares—if I would spread it on bread. You would hand me the silver knife, and I would leave. You would hand me the silver spoon, and I would leave. You would hand me the silver fork, and I would leave. You would ask me how I did it—how I swung hard enough to remove head from body like a wing from a moth, to cause a mark that we wanted to rub our fingers over. Let me teach you. Keep your eyes here. Watch. Watch the angle of the elbow, the position of the wrists. Let me show you how I will bring you to your beds.

BOSS BATTLE: THE DEATH OF THE CATERPILLAR

When I arrived the music changed—silent except for the sound of
a thousand legs shuffling—the ticking and scratching magnified by
close walls and the floor below. Your legs are long and frail and curl
under your body when you bend them to make yourself small—to
pretend that you are less than what you are, that you are making a
table for your body to rest upon. Your legs are smoother than this
most days, you assure me, as you kick and swirl with no regard for
where I am: a flick of a foot, a pulling up of a knee to your chin as if
you are thinking about where everything is heading; how you can fold
in on yourself, how you can knock me spinning to the floor.
But as with everything, a pattern emerges. But as with everything,
you turn left first, you turn left always, swing one leg over another
to greet me, your eyes red, your eyes blind, split and erased like a
hot stone, your head where your heart has been. You are tired of
dancing. You are tired and so you stop moving, feet flat against the
floor, and I am still as well, legs and arms slowed, knees straightened
stiff. Your ankles become wrists, the bottoms of your feet soften to
cupped palms. Where before I could place you in my mouth, now you
are on the air, wings larger than you've ever dreamed of, waking up
with air in your throat, a mess of limbs. You are large and it frightens
you. You are large and you frighten you so you flap your wings toward
my face, your body pulsating, fluttering, there and then gone. You will
be dead in three days, so I let you brush against my eyelashes, against
the bridge of my nose. You will be dead in three days, so there is no
lid on the jar.

TETRIS

We do not know what's at the top—where anything is coming from. Everything is falling.

My breath would be sucked back into my body and I would fall forever.

I would grow old.

My fingernails would grow until I bit them off.

My hair would grow as I fell.

I would rip the hair from my scalp and tie knots.

I would sing a song to pass the time. I would find a way to fall asleep with nothing but air to sleep on. I would lose weight.

I would bite the back of my hand. I would remember the eyes of my father until I forgot them.

Once, I told people that I fell off of a roof. I landed on my feet and everyone was amazed. I was lucky, they would exclaim. I know. I would be hugged. It would be a miracle. It would happen on the fourth of July while we watched fireworks over the beach. I wanted to know where the light went when it disappeared. I thought it would fall on us like leaves. I wanted to touch it, to put it in my pocket, to show everyone I knew. I could not do this. I could not do this so I told everyone I fell off a roof and survived. Everyone wanted to know how it felt when I landed and I would not know what to tell them. I tell them I don't remember. I remember the fall, the feeling of weightlessness. It was nothing like flying. I am not a bird. I am not a balloon. If a balloon lands in front of my house, I get candy. My parents would get a bottle of champagne. They would not drink it. It would sit underneath the sink until we have company who want to celebrate something.

I want to hit the bottom. I want my bones to break. This is a new way to get even—to make all things horizontal and make all things disappear. I would dream of lying at the bottom of a coffin in the cemetery behind my school. I could imagine not hearing. It would be dark but I could see my bones, see what I could become. Hold still. I understood the duration of forever. Hold still. My cousin is buried in a cemetery near Pennsylvania. My cousin's name fits inside my name. His name is part of my name. We leave a plant on his grave. When we do this we are standing over a baby. There is a bench with his name on it and people he has never met sit on it to rest their feet. I do not talk to him here.

When we leave the cemetery my father tells me not to put him in the ground.

Sometimes I would climb the bookcase at the foot of my bed, screaming. I used to sleep in a bed that was shaped like a boat. We filled the bookcase with books so I couldn't fit my feet on the ledges, so I wouldn't think that I could escape when I was asleep. In my dreams, there was blood. In my dreams, shapes fell from the sky. My father would run away from them as they fell behind him. I could see everything from my bed. He would die only to reemerge like a prophet, like a failed attempt. He would be crushed.

Most nights, I could not sleep.

My father would hold his hand against my head but I could not feel it. He falls asleep faster than I do. I am not good at these things. My weight will crush my father and I am sorry. When he thinks I am asleep he will leave. I cannot make things fit. I cannot prevent this from happening.

I need to know what's at the top. I think there might be trees like in the woods behind our house. I would return home with a piece of the plant in my finger—you could see through my skin. If I touched my thumb to it I could feel the heat of the wound. I would hold my hand underwater until the skin started to soften.

MEGA MAN 2

The egg that cracks is made of metal. The birds that escape from inside
are made of metal too: their wings sharpened by tools, a gear where
a lung should be, their bones hollow. The frog's mouth opens like a
knight's helmet—gravity swinging the jaw open like a breadbox, a bolt
bore through its fat gullet. You have swallowed your children: they
jump out and over my head like the sound of your ancestors, the sinews
in their legs replaced with the gears in the watch my mother gave me.
Before the city, before they stacked family on family like a blank through
a die, we could hear the frogs call out to each other while we tried to
sleep: you on top of me like a thin sheet of foil, your edges molded to
meet mine. This process is performed with difficulty, with caution, with
sacrifice. All of the pieces were marked out: you prefer oil and Prussian
blue, but I am not an engineer—I do not know how to measure the
flatness of things. I know that your cheek is concave and your calves are
not. I will use violet to mark out the rough parts for further machining.
I would mix the violet with resin, but the insects too are no longer
organic. We cannot finish the violin. We cannot touch the apple—we will
cut it into small, curved pieces. The worm in the apple is made of copper
pipe. The worm has eyes. The worm can blink.

We have lost everything. I can't tell you when it happened, but I knew
it would happen. We ran out of numbers for X. It will be strange
being home: I will stand on top of the buildings and my hair will
move. I will change color in the future. My body will collapse in on
itself—it will turn into a stick of gum and shoot skyward like an eleva-
tor, like the lift we stood in silent. When the carriage slows, jump.
If the timing is right, you will freeze in the air like a hummingbird,
like a dying spark. I should have stopped time—to have you in the
air forever. These types of things are not meant for the ground. This
is why I chose violet—to stop all of this from happening. I can make
night here: I can bring the stars inside. Here, in the future, there will
still be night. We do not know how to stop the earth from spinning
yet—to keep the sun on the tops of our round heads while the rest of
the world sleeps in darkness. What I thought were stars were shards
of glass. What I thought were shards of glass were shards of ice. It is
too cold here, I know.

Tell me where to go from here. To the left, fire. To the left, we remem-
ber walking down to the pond and watching the frogs jump into the
water when we stamped our feet near the edge. To the left, where this
all began: a factory, a magnet. In the future, you didn't exist yet: you
appeared in order to finish a phrase, to make this about more than
saving the world that someone created. To save the world made of
metal is not enough. There are machines in the woods. There is you
to think about.

Scrape away the metal on my stomach to reveal a narrow line for
marking. Line me up—use the window ledge as your guide. Cut a

hole in my body. Circle cutters make round holes. Attach the blades and oscillator.

This is the building we will live in when the future comes. I will keep you from overheating. This is the bed we will sleep in. There will still be night. This is where we will go from here—we will go up. We will walk on top of clouds but it will still be raining—the water will pour upward through the floor. Read the song of the birds, the great light dawning. Think of the frogs. Don't worry. In the future, we can eat the copper worm. We can drink the oil cold. We can compress the fillings and drop them from the sky. In the future, the metal will not rust in the rain. Keep the fan rotating. Keep nothing that reminds you of skin. Keep things moving. Keep thinking how you used to spin me by hand. Keep me level and feed me to the saw.

SAVE POINT: THE CHURCH

We all know they took the crosses out—the word synonymous with execution, the hanging of things and the beginning of other. They replaced them with looped tops as if they were children with no legs, a flower without its petals, an ear with no skin connecting it to a face. It would be silly to think that you would wait here for me, hands clasped in front of your navel, the ability to heal with the rose in your cheeks. When I return after uprooting every garden, you are gone, replaced by a hard bed that will heal my wounds by sunrise.

TECMO SUPER BOWL

The sun is not down and yet we are ready. Above our heads it is black
like the beeswax and carbon smeared beneath my eyes to block the
glare of the sun: the world will remain grey until I wipe it off of my
skin, until I rub the paraffin into my cheeks to stretch the blackness,
until my face turns grey like the sky, grey like smoke from a blackened
cork. Believe me when I tell you that if something was in the air I
would catch it. I would take a photograph as it spiraled, my palms the
shutter, my fingers the flash. All will be still, all things frozen, like
an egg in midair, like the moon faint against the silver. When I was a
child I had no one to throw the ball to. My mother asked me once if I
would like a brother or a sister, and I said yes. My mother, the twirler
of fire: the flipping of metal into the air only to have the baton float
down unchanged from its trip skyward. My father, the leader with
a broken wrist. My father the passed over—my father the eraser on
the last day of the season. My father with roses. My father working
late to build us a house. The sun setting before he got home. I am
sorry I broke everything. I am sorry I broke everything when I was
born. When I was born I broke everything. When I was born there
were cords around necks, there was a tear, there was a broken arm.

Before I take a photograph of what is left of the sun, I run to it as it
falls, my arm at my side while the other swings like a heavy chain,
like white gold. Before it grew too dark to see, I would throw the
ball to myself: left arm slung over my head at a beautiful angle, legs
creeping forward to catch up to the trajectory. To throw and to catch
at once: all things contained like a twisting loop, all energy within.
Someday I would throw the ball too far. Some days the ball would
bounce off of my fingers, bending them backward and toward my
body before springing back to where they once were: red and swollen
from the cold air. Once the bone did not bounce back: it popped like a
flashbulb, it barked like a called signal. I don't know why I am telling
you this. I don't know why I am telling you this because you cannot
picture me as anything but what I am: knuckles jagged, shoulder stiff
like the ground. You picture me faceless and young: helmet over ears,
pads peeking out from stretched collars, blood lost in slow motion
from a jarring blow, tips of gloves rubbing the red into the skin to
stop the bleeding, to prevent streaks of blood from staining my white
socks. When the season begins again, it begins again: me, much older
now, you, the same age. This is what you dream about, you say, that
it has taken me this long, that it has been the same year repeating,
the same rhythm in steps, the same blue eyes looking downward.
You told me once about you, spinning. You told me that when it was
time for you to be caught there was no picture taken with fingers and
palms—you had come quickly into the body and fell to the ground.
There was no lucky bounce, there was no good roll: your spine
cracked like an open book. You tell me that you would have been
there, screaming my number as the wind hardened my scabs. You tell
me that you can make my name rhyme with anything: apple, bow,

132

arrow. While you sleep, I will count the bones that curl up to your neck. I will look for ridges, a small X where they cut you open. I see nothing but skin. I will try to make my fingers match the gaps in the architecture, to feel the god of what is missing, to run my fingers over the shells, one after another, one after another, another, another, until I understand that you would have fallen through my hands and fallen flat, that your body would be smudged grey by the black grease. That I cannot catch you if I did not throw you. There is not enough time.

GHOSTS 'N GOBLINS

Here are the mistakes I made. There is a ghost in the window. There is a ghost in the mirror. There is a ghost in the mirror, close your eyes, say his name, he said, he repeated. Here is an error: here is a string, this is the end, here's a ship. The first mistake is that we thought it would lead us somewhere, on cemeteries and buildings and buildings in soft hard brick, churches touching the body, one hand on something other than a lance. I am nothing but a knight. I am nothing but a knight: dull as a bruised apple, like the rungs of a metal ladder, like a foot counting each error, like length of hair, like scratching nails. This story is a happy ending. This story is a happy error: an embrace without words, a silent error. We can reduce each other to bones in a box. When we are old, we throw our screens: we will not return to the house above them, we will not be found below. We tear our bodies, we tear, we will want to start from scratch. This room is an illusion. This room is a trap.

Shut your eyes, say his name, he said, he repeated. There is an error: here is a wire, here, finally, here is a ship. I'm nothing but a rider of a metal ladder: rungs as slow as a bruised apple, a counting error of leg, like nails scratching on the length of hair. This story has a happy ending. This story has a happy mistake: to embrace without question, a dumb mistake. Bones in a box, we can reduce to one another. When we're old, we throw our screens, we will not go home with them, we will not be found below. We will tear your body: in tears, we'll want to start from scratch. The room is an illusion. This room is a trap.

All mistakes are made in here. Is there a ghost in the window. Is there a ghost in the mirror. Is there a ghost in the mirror, here is a rope, here goes, here is a ship. The scraping of the nail. This story has a happy ending. This story has a happy mistake—press a finger to the metal in the body, hot like an oven in a color as orange as the bottom. How we must embrace without question, a dumb mistake with branches from each other, and we saw the dead as we were reaching. We're old, we'll throw his shield: we will not come home at the top, we will not be found under. We will tear them from our bodies, we will take off, we'll make love out of nothing organized as we swing to the ghosts. Start a mosaic of glass, not stone, brick, wood, fur, not scraping the floor of the wheels. No transparency: we can win as we move our body down our swords. We are the past, we are us, we are our own. This is our first mistake: a piece of bread as a sore tooth, a chunk taken out of our legs and spit on the green ground. We believe in this. We still believe. There are specters coming through the floor, violet, they should be here with us.

I am not here to talk about dirt. I'm not here on earth to let it under my nails, no strange lavender, no scratching the dirt to find some-thing to talk about. It is a mistake, a mistake. It is waiting there

with my face as tears: here is the color of my skin with a piece of
paper. Make it perfect. Here, my hair a dark shade: crescents in tears,
as I am the moon. Forget sand. You want to cast death. How difficult
is the day. How difficult are my eyes, larger than evil. About my red
shirt. About elections. The room is an illusion. This room is a trap.
I did not raise this ground. You changed me to make a paper on the
table, cook the rice boy sitting next to me: this is no way that we can
start again. You lie flat on my bed and tell me how her hand got in
trouble when I dream, you tell me how to take his place in the park.
To all those people who lost everything: it's my fault.

This room is an illusion. This room is a trap.

Here are the mistakes I made. There is a ghost in the window. There
is a ghost in the mirror. There is a ghost in the mirror, close your
eyes, say its name, say it again, say it again. Here is a mistake: here
is a rope, here is the end, here is a ship. The first mistake is the fact
that we believed this would lead us somewhere—out of graveyards
and buildings and into hard brick, a church, the touching of bodies,
a hand on something other than a lance. I am nothing but a knight. I
am nothing except a knight: dull like a bruised apple, like the rungs
on a metal ladder, like a foot counting each error like lines in sand,
like the length of hair, like scraping nail against nail—to smooth, to
make all things even. This story is a happy end. This story is a happy
mistake: to make metal break from body at the press of a finger, to
make it explode off of ourselves like a firework, like an orange in the
oven, like the folding of letters. Like an embrace with no words, like
a silent mistake. If we could cut ourselves on the edges, we could

arrange what is left of our fingers into notes—we could jump on top of gravestones like we are waiting to be divided: we could slash at each other with branches while the dead watched and reached out to us like we are glazed over and patched together, like bones in a box. When we are older we will throw our shields: we will not come home on top of them, we will not be found beneath them. We will rip them from our bodies, we will tear, we will make want out of nothing. My fingers were too large for scissors, for knives—knuckles swollen from mistiming: a car door shut early, a mask where a heart should have been, my clothes taking me with them like a hand held through a crowd of strangers—we move as the ghosts sway. This is the beginning of a mosaic—glass, not tile, not stone, not the scraping of fur, wood making wheels on the floor. There is transparency here: we flicker as we move, our swords below our bodies to let the ghosts know we exist—that we are ours, that we are our own. This is our first mistake: teeth along the sides of a piece of bread like a wound, like a chunk taken out of our feet and spit onto what we believe to be green—what we believe to be still. My fingers are not meant for this—the grooves in my thumbs are sore from overuse, blistering like heat over friction, like division—the removal of self from self. My father—he lived in a house that no longer exists, a ghost of a house, a body hurt by cold, by an end. I too lived in a house that no longer exists: shutters painted green instead of blue—where my bed was, a table with flowers on it, orchids maybe, tulips, never. There used to be a garden I called mine: violets coming through the ground like specters, like they are supposed to be here among us. I am not here to talk about dirt. I am not here to talk about scratching at the ground, the lavender by the handful, the dirt beneath my fingernails. This is a mistake—this is all a mistake. Here is a piece of paper the color of my skin: tear the shape of my face out from it—it is there waiting. Make it perfect. Make it as round as reason. Here, a darker shade for my hair: tear it into crescents, make me like the moon. Forget the ears. I have no mouth and I must tell you things: about how the picture of your arms makes me want to hold them by the wrists, to swing you like an axe, to throw you at the dead, to throw you to death. About the mistakes I have made, about the moments where I hover in the air, about how I must be able to go higher, about again, about more, more. About the loss of days and how none of this is difficult—there are my eyes, one larger than the other. About my shirt, red because that is all that's left—about choices. About choices. This room is an illusion. This room is a trap. The paper doll that is me is not me— this is something that I created: it was not grown like the tulips, I did not pull it up by the bulb to hand to you like a scepter, like a dagger. I did not raise it from the ground. This is something that you must believe—that this is not starting over. That there is no way that we can start over: you bringing a boy made out of paper to replace me, to sit the drawing at the table and cook it rice. About how you will lay him flat in his bed and hold his jagged hand when he dreams about me again, about how I am in the garden waiting to take its place. About how we used to have a house and how the bed he is in was in a different room: a room with flowers and chairs. About how I am gone now and not coming back. About how there is nothing to worry about—about how if I could, I would make another face where my body has been: that I would be smiling like the first day of everything, about how everything so far has been about the end of the world. About how everything so far has been about those who have lost everything. About how everything was so far from those who have lost everything. That this is my mistake. That this is the return. That this is happening again.

BOSS BATTLE: THE GIRL I WAS SUPPOSED TO SAVE

When I arrived the music changed—

and so did you.

FRIDAY THE 13TH

I am going to scare you like you've never been scared before. This is
not a letter home. This is not me telling you that there are rocks here,
fire. This is not an explanation of why this world is dark, why I can't
hear you when you call my name after the pills have been counted
and divided into boxes, into cylinders the color of a dying pumpkin,
of a shrimp dropped in oil. This is not a union. This is not the bring-
ing together of what was once a star and is now a statue that moves
when the light hits it, about life, about things bigger, faster. This
has nothing to do with any of this: of a loaf of bread, of the woman
behind the counter who rolls pennies, about the woman with no
legs, about the woman with one eye. It has nothing to do with any
of this. It is about yesterday. Yesterday, I walked home, I did this, I
did another thing, I am sparing you the details, I will spare you the
details. You and I know that I always tell you the details: me sitting
on the edge of a bed with blue sheets telling you the plot of a film I
had seen without you, stopping and restarting—I would forget to tell
you about the mother, the trees that could talk, the fat kid that made
us laugh, the game they lost, the wolves that chased. You could have
seen it for yourself—you would not need me to be your eyes, to shove

kernel after kernel into my mouth by the handful. I should tell you that this is not what I wanted to see—I should never look at these things: I would laugh at the boy who could not tell a lie, smile when the grown-ups would fall for his tricks. I have never been that clever. This is not a letter telling you about when I would stick a suction cup arrow in my mouth, about how I loved the pull on the back of my teeth, about how it caught the back of my throat once, how it looked like the perfect shot: mouth open, face split open like an orange—the marksman would have applauded—no need for a pen knife through a throat while sleeping, no need for any of that.

Afternoons, we would go to the store: we would start at the right and work our way left—I would put an onion in a plastic bag, I would put a nickel in a tin box for a caramel. I would never take more than one. I would smooth the sugar over my tongue. I could not talk. This is what happens: an endless list of horrible things. At the end, at the right, we would wait and I would read descriptions of worlds created, creatures I had never seen—there would be pictures of fear in motion, never more than two—women screaming, men with hands bursting out of their stomachs, fingers falling off the bone like melting popsicles, eyes widened, always widened. This is how information passed—I am the only son—no one would tell me about the loss of things, the time where the insect laid eggs in the woman's mouth, the man with knives for fingers. Here—let me tell you about something—about wings breaking through skin, about becoming the other. Let me tell you what happens when things go wrong. This is what happens when things go wrong. You and your friends are dead. You and your friends had names. The names: read them aloud like off a sheet of paper. The names: like someone has crossed them off in red, like we are floating dead in a river Like a sleepyhead dreaming of a new party. This is what I would do: if I had no hands, I would never stop wishing that despite having no fingers to wrap around all I hold dear—a rock, a hand—that I will get what I need: a piece of ice, a telephone, a knife slicing through skin with good intentions and the best directions—my hand outstretched like I'm asking for a dog to lick my hand before the camera shows the skin cut open: fur where there should not be fur, all things red. This is not me telling you these things: about pushing a rock down a hill because we wanted to change worlds, to make the landscape ours, to let the world know we were here, that we are here. This is what happens when you look in the water. This is what happens when we hear something about darkness, about chanting, about having to touch peeled grapes, about dried apricot halves, about floors that stick. This is the letter home. This is what happens when you ignore all of the children. The children, they are frightened. They disappear like breaths from mouths, like a lost sweater. You have ignored all of the children. You ignored all of the children. They disappear here:

BLASTER MASTER

This is what was left to us. I don't remember what I saw: the peeking out of legs from a hole we dug in the backyard, the wheels, the mountain. I live in the shadow of a mountain: colossal, a volcano dormant, something waiting to fill our heads with ash, to teach us what heat is. We used to dig in the yard: first with our hands and then with small spades and shovels. We would cut through the frozen ground, dirt under our fingernails, our pants damp from melted snow. We would dig until we could see the other side of Earth. We would dig through the core of everything: we would feel the fire, and the snow would melt—our beds would no longer be cold from the chilled glass, the windows surrounding my body as I slept. We would dig until we touched the roots of plants in another world: plum flowers and Chinese lilies. It would be a secret—flowers long dead from the snow pulled from some magic elsewhere, a hole in the ground marked by a piece of wood used to measure the height of the tomato vines, vines long since shriveled and iced over. In the hole we put reminders of ourselves. Here is a newspaper. Here is a piece of chocolate. Here are instructions on how to build a table—we will need all of these things when we are older. We will dig them up when our parents have gone,

when another family moves into our house—lies on our floors, spits
in our sinks. They will paint the shutters. They will replace the door.

When you are gone, who will drive the car. who will turn the wheel,
who will know where to turn. Who will draw the maps—straight
lines becoming sharp curves: all things to scale, all things considered.
When I was a child I read all of the books. I read about countries
that no longer exist and worlds that never did. I read about a boy like
me gone missing. I read about how he would leave words scrawled
in chalk for his mother to find: to let her know that he is still alive,
hiding in the garden, hiding in the river. Here is everything I have.
Here is the sound I will make, the song I will sing to let you know
that I mean what I say. I am learning the patterns of words because
I cannot imagine you gone; I cannot imagine what you have left. My
car will not move: it will sit still for days because I do not know what
to do. You have taught me, but I do not know what to do. I know
the wires, red and black, I know the patterns and the orders but I
need you to tell me. I am a frog. I am a frog, motionless. While I
was learning to live without you, someone pushed me into the road.
Someone pushed me into the road and laughed—my white shoes you
bought for me, caked in mud. Who will buy me new shoes—I will go
on without them despite hating the look of my feet. I will cut each
toe off, one by one, left to right. You will not be there to stop me, and
there is nothing I can do. When I was learning to live without you,
someone released the brake. The car rolled down the hill, backward,
away from where you sat. The wheel over my leg left no mark but
the ground did—red where white used to be, pieces of gravel stuck
in the wound. This is not what I wanted to take with me. I could not

take you with me so I took the ground instead, gravel harder than
early evenings in winter. I saw you hunched over the sink, crying for
my lost skin, and I turned away. I saw you again, eyes blue like mine,
and I told you that I was okay: if I die, don't put me in the hole with
the flowers. You said, Don't say these things. You tell me what to
keep when you die: the furniture in the foyer, the heirloom pieces,
the slant-top desk with the bookcase. You tell me the golf course,
the hole for your ashes. In the hutch in the room where we drink tea
is everything I need when you are gone: lists and names, numbers,
things left unsaid. In my dreams, the frogs by the pond are all dead—
their throats frozen shut. In my dreams I turn the latch to the cabinet. In
my dreams there is nothing inside: a hole burned in the wood where
something once was. Something that would tll me where to dig.
Something that would tell me what flowers to bring. Something that
would tell me what to do next.

BOSS BATTLE: MY BROTHER WHO CONTROLS THE WEATHER

When I arrived, the music changed—all notes go silent: the only thing audible is the hum of a soft rain, constant though we are inside, and for a moment it is peaceful, something we can sleep through, something that makes us turn off everything else so we can hear water on windows, on slanted roofs. You appear in a flicker, fast strobe first, then slowing to a gentle spin, arms outstretched and palms upward like you are receiving something. Someone who loves you will place a gumdrop into your hand so you can close your fingers around the jeweled sugar and place it between your teeth in a dirty scarfing.

This is where the lightning starts: dry heat from the sky and into your hands, leaving burn marks on skin, smoothing over heart lines like you have no heart, though I know it is there. The bolts, jagged like raised veins, come together in front of your stomach and slice toward where I am standing speechless. The outcome is uncertain: the voltage runs over my body like a pulped orange, turning everything I am into something I am not. Or it doesn't. The current springs back to you, knocking your helmet off of your head to reveal a face like mine, or it doesn't. The wind changes direction: I know this because I cannot stand still—I must pick up what is left, I must hold your blackened hands. I know this because for once I can see the rain slanted down-ward: falling in grey lines like the ghosts of our loved ones shooting toward the earth.

SAVE POINT: HOT SPRINGS

It is always about water: water is not here. Watch out, there is water. There is nothing left but water. You invite me to the lake and I do not respond: I remember what happened there—dogs that were not mine paddle furiously to keep their snouts above the break, ears flat against the sides of their slick heads. I am a dog: heat lashing out from my body, eyes made of black glass that makes you pretend to see something inside other than a reflection of you, a reflection of the reverse horizon—a negative, a face split in two. Show me a dog that understands love and I will call you a liar: these dogs are deaf, these dogs are simply swimming. Dogs die in hot cars. Dogs die in bath-tubs; dogs die in open water. Dogs die first. Dogs are the last things remaining. I knew a dog that jumped off the cliffs and cracked its head open on a hidden rock. The dog floated, a mass of skin and hair, a dead dog's float. I knew of a dog that froze to death. I knew of a dog that was bit by a snake, right on its cheek, the snake unwavering in its path down the river. I do not respond to your invitation. I do not respond to your invitation because if I did I would have to tell you these things: eyes open, tongues out, wilting in the sun like a rotting peach. I do not tell you these things because you love dogs, how they crawl up on couches, how they lick hands, how they make you safe, how you sleep next to them, how you set everything out for them, one thing next to another, how you make sure they are properly fed, how they are drinking enough water. I do not tell you these things because of the way I say the word *water*, fast and muddled, like it is caught in my mouth, like there is no bite to it: water, water, water, watermelon, waterweight, waterfall, watermoccasin. I do not tell you these things because by telling you these stories and pretending these things happened to dogs I am not saving you from anything. I am not saving you from the fact that children die in hot cars, that children die in bathtubs, that when someone they love dies we tell them the loved one is sleeping, that they have passed out, blacked out. That when their dog dies we tell them that they have run away. That they still love us, but they are gone now. That when they die they are sleeping. That the water is too hot. That the water is too cold. That the water is just right and I am sorry I cannot come to the lake because the dog you love is not a dog and it is not a child and it is not me. That the bottom of my feet cannot touch the bottom. That I cannot afford to be taken by the ankles.

THE FINAL BOSS

When I arrived, the music changed, and then it went silent—nothing of note except the ringing in my ears, the residue of the clinking of a glass, the dropped phone call, the silence of a house in the morning. There is nothing romantic about the idea of final when final arrives like this: not with an arrow in the eye, not with a body losing grip on the floor and disappearing in the dark with a sparkle and a wink, not with a final blink after turning magenta, a red not found in nature, a red not found in your face, not even while choking, not even while gasping for breath. What you have imagined the final stage to be is not what it is—here is a list of what it is not. It is not surrounded by family and handwritten cards from friends, fresh flowers replacing dead flowers, no, never dead flowers, get them out of here, cast them into the street, put them in another room, the water will not save you. It is not done loudly, a body on fire, a spine crushed, speed meeting its opposite, the flavor of tin on the tongue, a lost tooth. It is not done by saving. It is not done by returning to saving, it is not done by holding, our bodies taken out of the world and back into our world, body slouched in a sofa, wrist cracked, skin on the thumb worn thin by being anyone except ourselves: a bird, a boy, a knight, a woman who can jump to the moon, a man in a car we will never see, the hand of a god we love. You asked for it, and here it is: you will fall asleep and you will not wake up. You will drown inside yourself—what is in you will want to leave you through your mouth and up your throat, to crawl from under your tongue and onto your pillow and into the blades of the ceiling fan, repeating, repeating, repeating. You will not repeat anything, you will not be able to start over, start at the room where you arrived when the music changed, start at the room before the room where the music changed, where the music

153

was the same as it ever was, the same melody that makes you think of oranges and small dogs and mistakes that you made in the past: the girl you kissed you never should have kissed, the girl you kicked you never should have kicked, your mother, your father, the smoke in your lungs on nights where it was too loud to hear what you were saying, the awfulness in your chest. You have eaten all the cake, you have eaten all the jewels, you have put your hands to the sides of every princess, and this is where it ends, you can watch if you'd like, you can see the numbers counting back from ten, like the celebration of a new year, like you will shove twelve grapes into your mouth and you will chew, breaking through the skin of the fruit to get to the sweetness, to choke them down, one for every new second, so you can make your first wish of many wishes, for the princess to be safe, for the health of your friends, for happiness, when you should have wished you would not die. That your parents would not have to bury you after years of telling you that they would not be burying you, that you let it slip that you wish that they would burn your bones and let your ashes escape into the atmosphere, that your dust would become stars because you do not know how stars work, that you, stupidly, sloppily, could become something larger than yourself when you are dead. Anything but a hardened heart and the shortness of breath and the lament of a long walk wasted and a good life spoiled. Before you go to sleep, you swallow everything: more air, more water, things to make your blood work harder, ways to stop you from thinking these thoughts—that your breaths would be deeper than the coldest lake, that all of the lights would stop spinning, that if you had another chance you would write all of this down so you, you, whoever "you" is, could follow it tirelessly, endlessly, that you could walk through this life as you walk through yours, that you could make it this far, that you could do it better. That by the time you get to the room where there is no music there would be no glass in your veins, that the color of your heart would not be the color of a king but the color of the final flag raised—the final, the final, the final. This is what you asked for and this is what you will have: something larger than you, something rain-soaked and wet like a new child, something evil, something that can read your thoughts, something that is a thing inside a thing inside of a thing like a nesting doll, something that sprouts wings, something that was you once, smiling with a white tooth and a kind eye, something that is you but made of magic. Something magic.

GAME GENIE

And what if we could come back. And what if none of this meant
that this, all of this, was a life wasted, that there were words that
could somehow live inside us like worlds, that I could pretend that
there was nothing here but different colors than those I am used to:
colors that don't exist in nature or whatever this is, this nature that
has been created here, but colors that remind me of hospitals, colors
that remind me of the river bottoms or a shirt you once wore that
I will never see again. Sometimes these colors are numbers: letters
left without any attachment, symbols of static. When I hear the right
tone, I see colors. This, plus this plus this equals blue. When you
whisper into my ear the way I see the world changes—like it never
existed like this before, like your dog never died and your father
never left and you never forgot me. What was meant was not what
was meant. We could swim through the air. There is fire underwater.
Time will not move for us; it will remain at nine repeating, nine over
and over, nine like the number means something. The numbers mean
nothing. The numbers mean the color white and I am sorry that I
don't remember what they are. There is a combination of letters and
numbers that will give me everything. There is a combination of letters

and numbers that will let me carry the moon. There is a combination
of letters and numbers that will let me break you into pieces with just
one swing of my hand, that will make me invisible, that will make me
forget the word *risk*, that will put an end to all of these things. You
look better with purple hair. You look better with your arm missing,
with your arm replaced by a rectangle, with a beanstalk that reaches
toward the sky yet brings home nothing: no coins, no giant at the top
asking me to lead the life I should have led before any of this hap-
pened, no lesson to be learned about what any of this means. I know
there is a hand and I know there are letters here. I know that if I put
them together I can change things: I can walk backwards and you can
laugh, that bodies aren't supposed to move like this, that my swollen
ankles are pretending all of this is meant to be, that all of this is natu-
ral, that the wind is taking me places I have never been. That I could
jump higher. That if I fell down I would come back new, come back
alive, come falling through the ceiling like a rocket, like rain on your
head, like fireworks, like every light ever shone. That I could peek
into your world with eyes that were once mine, that I could cut a hole
in a wall, that I could poke my head through. I don't know what let-
ters I should use. I don't know the spell. I don't know how to wish
for more wishes. I don't know how any of this works and so I change
the color of your hair. I give myself a gun, and another gun, and an-
other gun. I give myself all of the coins in the world. If I find a coin on
the ground and put it in my pocket it will disappear like you did, like
you should have done, like you did a long time ago. This is something
that I never told you. In my dreams, they all come back: you in a
place that we know exists somewhere but not anywhere, you wearing
something you would never wear, a color divided in half, a devastating

red. You wrap your arms around my throat and bury your face in my
body and you whisper me things: the names of colors, where you
wish you were, where you wish we were, that we could be swimming,
that there were fountains, that if I waved my hand a brick would
appear instead of fire, that you could run into me, touch my skin
and not be poisoned, not fall from this world like a dead duck, like
a broken dance floor, like a rotten plant. That there were ways to do
this without running. That there were ways to do this without dying,
without reversing time, without starting over—that we could start
near the end, that we could start where we deserve, that we could
skip everything that means nothing, that we could forget how we got
here and how we grew and how I learned that your favorite color is
purple, how I learned your favorite color is green, how I learned your
favorite season is winter, how you love to see me slide backwards
like there are words made of ice, like you can hear what half a heart
sounds like, like we can start where it is most difficult. This is where
it all comes back. This is where it begins, with you, and this is where
it ends. This is what I am telling you. This is something I will never
tell you: in my dreams, he comes back. In my dreams, I am sitting in
a kitchen that I sat in on the day he died. That it is his birthday and
we are eating potatoes and looking at greeting cards and he comes up
from the basement where we used to play and I am shocked to see
him as I remembered him, but taller, and everyone is unaffected—
that I am told to set the table, that I am told to stop eating peanuts as
dessert will be served soon, that there is a cake with his name on it
welcoming him back from the dead, like this sort of thing happens all
the time—that those we love choose to run heart first into bottomless
pits, into bullets, into fire, they drown, they touch spikes, they lose by

one basket and disappear, they leave notes for younger brothers not to walk into the house and to go across the street and call the police, that they wrap cords around their necks until they stop breathing, that someone tripped over a cord, that this is an accident, that things froze, that we have waited long enough to start again, and here we are, a year later and someone brought you back. Someone knew the letters. Someone knew the code. Someone knew the code and it was not me. Someone knows that we cheated: the colors greyed, our names misspelled. Someone knows we will be lost within the walls and stuck in the world. Someone knows. Someone knows that he is dead. I am awake, and you are not here. Someone knows that this is where it all resets.

ACKNOWLEDGMENTS

All Boss Battles and Save Points originally appeared in *Level End*, a chapbook released by Origami Zoo Press in 2012.

Sections from *Leave Luck to Heaven* appear in different forms in the following journals:

Simon's Quest, *The Collagist*
Zelda II: The Adventure of Link (as "Zelda Revisited"), *Conjunctions*
Super Mario Bros. 3, *Hotel Amerika*
Bubble Bobble (as "No Parasol Stars"), *Caketrain*
Super Mario Bros. & Ninja Gaiden Trilogy, *Hobart*
Double Dribble, *Sonora Review*
Adventure Island, *Metawritings: Toward a Theory of Nonfiction*
Punch-Out!!, *Barrelhouse*
Metroid, *Ghost Town*
Wizards and Warriors, *Bluestem*
Balloon Fight, *Parcel*
R.B.I. Baseball, *Fairy Tale Review*
Boss Battle: A Woman Made of Feathers, *Housefire*

Brian Oliu

Ghosts 'N Goblins, *Corium Magazine*
Donkey Kong, *Puerto del Sol*
Rampage, *Paper Darts*
Gradius, *Smokelong Quarterly*
Tetris, *Fix It Broken*
Maniac Mansion, *Tongue*
Boss Battle: My Brother Who Controls the Weather, *realpoetik*
Boss Battle: The One With the Long Neck, *elimae*
Save Point: Hot Springs & The Final Boss, *DIAGRAM*
Friday the 13th, *Los Angeles Review*
River City Ransom, *Necessary Fiction*
Rad Racer, *The Destroyer*
Shadowgate, *New South*
Dragon Warrior, *SundogLit*
Mega Man 2, *The NewerYork*
Kid Icarus, *BULL: Men's Fiction*
Tecmo Super Bowl, *Similar Peaks*
Super Mario Bros. 2, *Revolution House*
Blaster Master, *The Minnesota Review*
Goonies II, *Cartridge Lit*

I would like to offer thanks:

To editors who published these essays or commented on them graciously or critically: Matt Sailor, Drew Krewer, Nicole Walker, Lisa Summe, Jared Yates Sexton, Holly Harrison, Ann Beman, Brandon Hobson, Kate Lorenz, Dave Housley, Ander Monson, Micaela Morrissette, David Blumenshine, Rachel Burns, Michael J. Seidlinger, Riley

Michael Parker, Jared Lively, Greg Dybec, and all of the assistant editors who helped make these pieces fit for print.

To Mike Meginnis and Tracy Rae Bowling, for being incredible editors and for believing in this project. I am forever indebted to y'all. Thanks for everything.

To an amazing crop of teachers that I was truly humbled to study under: Lia Purpura, Jane Satterfield, Ron Tanner, Wendy Rawlings, Joel Brouwer, Michael Martone, and especially Kate Bernheimer.

Special thanks to colleagues (and twitterfam!) that have supported my writing, including Sal Pane, Roxane Gay, Cheryl Strayed, R.A. Villanueva, Kelly Davio, Justin Daughtery, Ian Denning, Gabe Durham, Aaron Burch, Joseph Michael Owens, Jill Talbot, Matt Bell, Tyler Gobble, Laura Relyea, Christopher Newgent, Aubrey Hirsch, and countless, countless other amazing folks.

To Sam Martone and Rebecca King, for publishing *Level End* and taking such care with it, as well as being such champions of writing.

To the best group of Player 2s anyone could ever ask for: Barry Grass, Abbas Abidi, Jason McCall, Tessa Fontaine, Farren Stanley, Jessica Richardson, Ryan Browne, John Wixted, Jessica Johnson, Matt Myrick, Meredith Noseworthy, B.J. Hollars, Colleen Hollister, Colin Rafferty, Tasha Coryell (xoxo), Andrew Farkas, John Wingard, Lisa Nikolidakis, Stacey Andeen, Joseph Wood, Rob Dixon, Andy Johnson, Laura Kochman, Austin Whitver, MC Hyland, Brooke Champagne,

Bob Weatherly, Alissa Nutting, Natalie Hopper, Rob Cramer, Kimberley Coughlin, Matt Parolie, Erin Hill, Whitney Holmes, Patti White, P.J. Williams, David Welch, Caitlyn Smith, Gerry Tobin, and other members of the Roll Tide Nation that I am forgetting to list.

To my amazing students and Slash Pine Press interns: it is an honor to be able to see you grow as writers and as people. Thanks for keeping me going. I am your biggest fan.

To Jeremy Hawkins, Lucas Southworth, Chris Mink, and Elizabeth Wade—I am so fortunate that the best readers of my work are some of the best friends I could ever hope for.

To Steve Kowalski, who inspired this collection in the first place. We the best.

To my family: especially Mom, Dad, Oma, Nan, Gramps, and Rebecca— as well as those I do not have the luxury to thank in person: Avi and Ian. These stories are yours as much as they are mine.

And finally to you, reader. Your quest has now ended.

BIO

Brian Oliu is originally from Readington, New Jersey, and currently teaches at the University of Alabama, where he is the associate director of the Slash Pine Press internship. He is the author of *So You Know It's Me* (Tiny Hardcore Press, 2011), a series of Craigslist Missed Connections; *Level End* (Origami Zoo Press, 2012), a chapbook based on videogame boss battles; and *i/o* (Civil Coping Mechanisms, 2015), a memoir in the form of a computer virus.